THOMAS GIRTIN
Genius in the North

David Hill
with an introduction by Susan Morris

HAREWOOD

Designated as a museum with an outstanding collection

Published in 1999 by
Harewood House Trust
Moor House, Harewood, Leeds LS17 9LQ

British Library Cataloguing in Publication Data.
A CIP catalogue record for this book is available from the British Library.

ISBN 1-899928-11-1 cloth
ISBN 1-899928-10-3 paperback

Title page: *Thomas Girtin – **Harewood Bridge** (exh. no. 22, detail).*

Typeset in 10.5/13pt Garamond
Designed and produced by
Andrew Esson, Baseline Arts Ltd., Oxford.

ACKNOWLEDGEMENTS:

The authors would like to thank the following for their kind assistance with enquiries: Tony and Caroline Cressey, Vivian Cartwright, Simon Fenwick, R.W.S, Ann Goodchild, Martin Gresswell, Lowell Libson of Spink-Leger, Anne Lyles, Charles McCaughey, Corinne Miller, Lord Normanby, Charles Nugent, Janet Skidmore, Kim Sloan, Henry Wemyss of Sotheby's, Scott Wilcox, Moira Wogan, Andrew Wyld of Agnew's, and all the curators and owners who have generously made work available for exhibition.

The exhibition was curated and organised at Harewood by Jane Sellars. Without her unfailing and enthusiastic application to all the hard work involved, and the support of Sally Wilks and Terence Suthers, Director of Harewood House Trust, the exhibition could not have taken place.

Printed and bound by
Raithby, Lawrence & Company Ltd.

Contents

*1. **Harewood House from the South East,** 1801 (detail)*

Harewood House Trust

One of Girtin's largest watercolours, for which Edward Lascelles paid twenty guineas. An outstanding example of the 'breadth' and 'genius' so much admired by Lascelles.

Foreword

THOMAS GIRTIN: GENIUS IN THE NORTH is the latest in a regular programme of exhibitions which explores the role of Harewood in the development and progress of English watercolour painting. The first was *Harewood Masterpieces: English Watercolours and Drawings* in 1995 which outlined the riches of the collection at Harewood and celebrated the creation of a unique environment for the display of watercolours at the house. This enabled us to display historic watercolours in the kind of setting for which they were originally designed, and did so, we hope, without contradicting the house as a home and an instrument for living and without turning it too consciously into a museum. The second exhibition in 1996 explored the watercolours by Charlotte, Viscountess Canning, aunt of my great-grandmother, and Lady-in-Waiting to Queen Victoria. Several albums of her drawings survive in the library at Harewood and we were able for the first time to present a selection of these to the public.

The last exhibition on the theme of watercolours was *Turner in the North of England, 1797* in 1997 which explored in detail the connection of the great painter with Harewood and celebrated the two hundredth anniversary of his tour of the north of England. Now we turn to Thomas Girtin, Turner's close friend and contemporary, who was likewise closely connected with Harewood during his formative years.

Girtin died in 1802 aged only twenty-seven. Turner – a generous but not unperceptive man – said 'If Tom Girtin had lived, I should have starved.' At the time of his death he stood with Turner on the threshold of fame. In fact he had already won the greater admiration from his fellow artists, and we can see that he had much influence on the younger generation of painters including John Varley, John Sell Cotman, Peter de Wint and Augustus Wall Callcott. All of these worked at Harewood and we hope eventually to explore the work of each of them. My ancestor Edward Lascelles, son of the first Earl, is even known to have declared a preference for Girtin over Turner, and to have had such a friendly relationship with the artist as to take lessons in painting from him, and to have kept a room at Harewood always ready for his use.

Although Girtin is famous among those who love English watercolours, he is almost unknown to the wider public. This is the clear result of his being neglected by scholarship in recent decades. The last major book devoted to him, by Girtin and Loshak, was published well over forty years ago in 1954. The last exhibition devoted to him in Britain was that held at the Whitworth Art Gallery, Manchester, and the Victoria and Albert Museum in London in 1975. The last exhibition anywhere in the world was that organised by Susan Morris at the Yale Center for British Art, New Haven, USA, in 1986.

It is clearly high time that his work be seen again. This is the first exhibition ever to focus on any particular aspect of Girtin's work. It is remarkable how many of his acknowledged masterpieces are north of England subjects, but this only serves to highlight the riches that are to be discovered in his work as a whole, and how much more work and research might fruitfully yet be done.

We hope that our exhibition will reawaken public interest in this quiet but profound artist. Perhaps we might stimulate some proper acknowledgement of his significance to mark the two hundredth anniversary of his death in 2002.

The Harewood House Trust is especially grateful to the British American Arts Association and Alton and Elizabeth Peters, who very generously supported the publication of this catalogue in honour of my own 75th birthday. We are also indebted to Bretton Hall College of the University of Leeds and the Paul Mellon Centre for Studies in British Art for the help they too have given to this publication. Finally, we thank David Hill, curator of the exhibition, for his new scholarship, and Susan Morris for her insightful contribution to this book.

Fig. I Harewood House from the South East.
(Photograph: David Hill)

Thomas Girtin

An introduction by Susan Morris

*2. John Opie – **Portrait of Thomas Girtin,** c.1800*
National Portrait Gallery, London

Aged about twenty-five, and possibly taken at the time of his marriage to Mary Ann Borrett in October 1800.

*3. **Dunstanburgh Castle, Northumberland, in a thunderstorm** c.1795.*
The Visitors of the Ashmolean Museum, Oxford

Made while still an apprentice, but already showing a keen appreciation of the potential of north country scenery.

TOM WAS A BRILLIANT FELLOW' muttered Turner to Thomas Girtin's relative Mr Jackson, when they chanced to meet at a dinner party early in the 19th century[1]. For a decade these two modestly-born Londoners – exact contemporaries, born in 1775 – chased each other up the scales of artistic achievement and the ranks of English patronage. But Girtin died, aged 27, on the brink of real fame, in 1802; Turner had another half century of achievement and honours before him.

The son of a Southwark brushmaker, Girtin came to the landscape of the north of England by the same route as Turner, through the antiquarian vogue for medieval ruins and ancient churches. In 1789 he was apprenticed to the topographical watercolourist Edward Dayes, an ambitious man, 'neither amiable nor happy'[2], who was to commit suicide in 1804. The youthful Girtin soon mastered Dayes's watercolour style: cathedrals and castles seen in close-up, undershadowed in grey and blue, and overtinted with local colours, mainly pastel pinks, yellow-green, pale orange – delicate 18th century topographical drawings. Dayes sometimes worked from the sketches of amateur artists such as the Cheapside linen-draper and keen antiquarian James Moore (1762-1799). That task, too, devolved on Girtin, and Moore became an enthusiastic early patron, struck by his talent and ebullient charm.

Moore toured Scotland in 1792 and working up his amateur sketches of subjects such as *Abernethy Round Tower* or *Dunstaffnage Castle* gave Girtin his first glimpse of the rugged architecture of the north and the legends and history surrounding it. His continuing work for Dayes and Moore over the next few years gave him ample opportunity to develop his ideas. His imagination was given particularly free rein in a watercolour of *Dunstanburgh Castle, Northumberland, in a thunderstorm* (exh no. 3).

By 1794 Girtin had been taken up by Dr Thomas Monro, a distinguished physician of mental

1. Quoted by the watercolourist John Joseph Jenkins (1811-1885), Secretary of the Old Water-Colour Society, in manuscript notes for a history of the Society, now in the possession of the Royal Water Colour Society, Bankside Gallery, London. Jenkins heard this anecdote on 12th July 1852 from Chambers Hall, who bought a large number of Girtin drawings (now mostly in the British Museum) from Mr Jackson, a wealthy timber merchant and father-in-law of Girtin's engraver brother John (Jenkins MSS: RWS J 39.14). Jenkins's manuscripts formed the basis of J.L. Roget's *History of the 'Old Water-Colour' Society,* 1891. I am grateful to Simon Fenwick, Archivist of the RWS, for drawing my attention to these manuscripts.
2. E Edwards, *Anecdotes of Painters,* London, 1808, p.285.

disorders and consultant to George III. Along with Turner, Girtin was set to copy drawings by John Robert Cozens, Thomas Hearne and Monro's Adelphi Terrace neighbour John Henderson. The young pair later told Joseph Farington that 'Girtin drew in outlines and Turner washed in the effects'[3] – a shrewd evaluation of their relative merits, for Turner's painterliness and Girtin's instinctive sense of composition and extraordinary, tensile hooked-and-dotted line were already apparent. Girtin stroppily complained that this division of labour did not allow him 'the same chance of learning to paint'[4]. In other respects, too, his training does not seem to have been all he might have wished. His relationship with Dayes does not seem to have ended sweetly. Dayes is accused of having set Girtin to the menial task of colouring prints. in order to retard his progress, and when the young genius rebelled, of having him jailed as a recalcitrant apprentice. If the story of the jailing is to be believed – and there is no concrete evidence – Viscount Malden had to buy out his indentures in order to release him[5].

In 1796 Girtin, free at last from his uneasy seven-year apprenticeship, made his first truly independent sketching tour, to Yorkshire, Northumberland and the Scottish Borders. The northernmost limit of this tour was probably reached on 11th October 1796 when Girtin (most unusually for him) dated a small pencil sketch of the *Village of Jedburgh, Roxburghshire,*[6] of which the lure was the magnificent Norman abbey. This tour was about the pursuit of medieval England: Girtin drew the churches at York and Ripon, and the castles at Barnard Castle and Richmond. Because, unlike Turner's, none of Girtin's travelling sketchbooks survive, it is difficult to reconstruct the precise route of his tours. He would return to favourite sites over several years, refining and reassessing. A comparison of the 1796 *Durham* (exh. no. 4)[7] with another dated 1799 (exh. no. 5)) shows Girtin's increasing concern for weight and monumentality in architecture.

On his 1796 journey Girtin explored the Yorkshire and Northumbrian fortresses and abbeys.

3. Farington Diary, 11th November 1798.
4. Roget i82.
5. Cf. G&L p.22 ff., where the story of the jailing is given a thorough quizzing.
6. G&L 166i, BM 1889-6-3-256. The drawing is inscribed '1796/ X / 11' This could also be read as 2nd October.
7. The basis of a large finished watercolour in the Victoria and Albert Museum, London (33-1928, G&L 159ii, V&A 1975 no. 17 not repr), and of a chiaroscuro study (Bacon collection, G&L 159I) which was probably made as a preliminary to the large watercolour.

4. ***Durham, Cathedral and Castle from above Framwellgate Bridge,*** *1796*
Birmingham Museums and Art Gallery

Probably a sketch from the 1796 tour, and possibly coloured on the spot.

These defiant and spectacular relics brought out for the first time the Romanticism of his work in watercolours such as the brooding *Richmond Castle* (exh no. 35) based on a lost 1796 pencil sketch. In this 1796 tour Girtin stuck close to the tried and tested topographical favourites – York, Ripon, Durham – which had for decades found a ready market in watercolours and prints. While most of his output was intended for London, he had probably already made the acquaintance of a few northern patrons. Family tradition has it that Girtin stayed with George Selby at Twizell, Belford, Northumberland: he certainly made a handsome drawing of nearby *Bamburgh Castle*[8] in the rich ochre and blue palette which he developed around this date, which remained with descendants of the Selby family until the 1920s. It is likely, however, that Girtin first encountered most of his patrons in the drawing rooms of Mayfair and St James's.

Though initially taken up by professional men such as Dr Thomas Monro, Girtin's patrons by the end of his career encompassed the cream of Georgian society. They had fortunes derived from land, from burgeoning industry, from the West Indies trade, from political acumen; some were Whigs, some were Tories. They were all caught up in the ferment of an extraordinary decade, the 1790s, when fears of French invasion and Radical agitation at home went hand-in-hand with cultural flowering – opportunistic snapping-up of the best European collections on the back of Revolutionary upheavals; staunch support of British watercolour, the most exciting medium of the decade, spearheaded by artists such as Turner and Girtin. Glimpsed viewing William Beckford's Altieri Claudes in 1799[9], the two young artists had plenty of opportunity to study the classical landscapes of Poussin and Claude, the deep autumnal tones and exquisite observation of natural effects of the 17th century Dutch masters, in the drawing rooms of patrons such as Sir George Beaumont and Charles Long.

'A delightful companion'[10] possessed of youth, talent, wit and charm, Girtin gained pupils in the

8. G&L 160 repr, ex Sotheby's 13 March 1980 (134 repr).
9. Farington *Diary*, 9th May 1799.
10. The assessment of Miss Hog, Girtin's wife's best friend and bridesmaid. Jenkins MSS RWS J 39/10.
11. Jenkins MSS RWS J 39/16.

grandest households, including the pretty, vivacious Lady Gower, Countess of Sutherland in her own right, heiress to a huge tract of northern Scotland. She was married to Lord Gower, a 'leviathan of wealth' who inherited the Bridgewater estates from his uncle and the Marquessate of Stafford from his father in 1803, and who was created Duke of Sutherland in 1833. The Gowers' patronage of contemporary British art was matched by a love of European Old Masters: in 1798 Lord Gower, with his uncle the Duke of Bridgewater and Lord Carlisle, bought the famed Italian and French painting collection of the Duc d'Orléans.

Many years later, the by now Dowager Duchess of Sutherland recalled to James Holland the unusual thoroughness of Girtin's teaching methods: 'he used to point out the time of the day, the cast shadows and particular effect suited to the time and scene &c – a mode of teaching far in advance of the time'.[11] The Duchess's remarks are a reminder of the acute naturalistic observation that underlies even his most rigorously 'classical' compositions. A serene view of *Kirkstall Abbey, Morning* (exh. no. 15) has hitherto been titled 'Evening' but is here retitled by David Hill as morning. It was paired in the collection of Girtin's son, the surgeon Thomas Calvert Girtin, with a watercolour of *Kirkstall Abbey, Evening* of the same size (exh no. 14). In pairing these two substantial 'morning and evening' subjects, Girtin was emulating the Old Masters who lined his patrons' walls:

Fig II. ***J M W Turner Durham Cathedral and Castle from above Framwellgate Bridge,*** *c.1798*
Royal Academy of Arts

5. ***Durham Cathedral and Castle from above Framwellgate Bridge,*** *1799*
The Whitworth Art Gallery, University of Manchester

Exactly the same view as painted by Turner (Fig. II).

remaking Claude for a new age and in a new medium.

Through teaching wealthy amateurs Girtin formed a network of contacts who bought his drawings, invited him to stay at their country houses and pushed his fortunes in the fiercely competitive London art world of the 1790s. After his 1796 northern tour, he spent the summer of 1797 touring Devon but seems to have gone north every summer for the rest of his life, with trips to Wales in 1798 with an artist called Moss and in 1800 with his patron Sir George Beaumont. One of the major reasons for his repeated visits to the north was the patronage of Edward Lascelles, eldest son of Lord Harewood. They seem to have first met around 1797, possibly through their common association with Viscount Malden of Cassiobury Park near Watford.[12] Malden was an early supporter of Turner and Girtin, and regularly plucked artists from the circle of Dr Monro, who had a house at Bushey not far from Cassiobury. He is credited with having rescued Girtin from his supposed confinement in prison. Lascelles visited Cassiobury frequently and possibly there developed his taste for the avant-garde. A more detailed account of Girtin's close association with Harewood is given by David Hill in the following section, 'Genius in the North'.

Probably in 1800, either on his way to or from Harewood, Girtin may have stopped at Nostell Priory near Wakefield, home of Sir Rowland Winn (1775-1805). The stub of a cut-out page in the Shepherd Sketchbook (Whitworth Art Gallery, Manchester) is inscribed by Girtin in the margin: 'Gravel caves with a peep of the sea. Sold to Miss Winn Nostel [sic] Priory. 1. 1s.'[13] He had perhaps stopped off at Nostell to give Miss Winn drawing lessons.

A near neighbour of the Winns, Sir John Ramsden (1755-1839) has recently been revealed as another important Yorkshire patron of Girtin. Ramsden lived at Byram Hall near Ferrybridge, a major coaching centre on the great north road, and was brother-in-law of Lord Rockingham of Wentworth Woodhouse. He was an MP in the Rockingham (Whig) interest from 1780-84 and typical of the artistically aware mid-18th century Yorkshire gentry. Like Edwin Lascelles at Harewood, he employed Carr of York and Adam at Byram; he was also an assiduous collector of Old Master paintings.

Between 1990 and 1992 a descendant of Sir John Ramsden sold four, hitherto-unpublished, late Girtin drawings, among the finest in existence: *Jedburgh Abbey from the South-east* (*c.*1800), *Mynnydd Mawr, North Wales* (dated 1799), *A Farmyard with Cattle* (*c.*1800) and *Lydford Gorge, Devon* (dated 1800).[14] In pristine condition, since they had been kept in portfolios since they were made, these watercolours reveal the rich palette of Girtin's work *c.* 1801, which can also be seen, despite darkening, in *Stepping Stones on the Wharfe* (exh. no. 18). This late palette encompasses lowering, deep indigo clouds; surprisingly bright and acid greens

12. Cf. Hill 1995 pp. 14, 28.
13. Whereabouts of drawing unknown. The Winns are not known to have owned any other Girtin drawings.
14. Sotheby's 11 July 1990 (92), 11 April 1991 (68), 9 April 1992 (41), and 11 July 1990 (91)
15. Sale of Sir John Ramsden, Bulstrode Park, Gerrards Cross, Bucks, Christie's 27th May 1932, lots 21 and 22. The former is G&L 355, V&A 1975 no. 65 repr, now National Gallery of Scotland, the latter G&L 318, sold Sotheby's 21 November 1985 lot 97 repr.
16. Two substantial watercolours, *Plymouth* (Ashmolean Museum) and *Devonport* (National Gallery of New Zealand, Wellington) are dated 1801. There is a pencil sketch of *Mount Edgecumbe,* Devon in the Shepherd Sketchbook.
17. Jenkins MSS RWS J 39/5. Miss Hog's words recounted to Jenkins by Girtin's granddaughter Mary Girtin in 1852.
18. Jenkins MSS, RWS J 39/14. Jackson's words recounted by Chambers Hall to Jenkins on 12th July 1852.

and yellow-greens, and russet-toned foregrounds. The sonority of colour rivals Turner's watercolours of this period, but Girtin's range is broader and more naturalistic.

Sir John Ramsden owned at least two more watercolours by Girtin: an 1800 view of *The Village of Jedburgh* and *A View on the River Taw looking from Braunton Marsh towards Instow and Appledore, Devon.*[15] It is obvious that although Girtin's northern patrons bought watercolours with personal, topographical associations, such as Lascelles's drawings of Harewood, they were more than willing to entertain other themes. Edward Lascelles also owned a beautiful sketch of an unidentified Devon estuary, drawn with the fluid economy of Girtin's late plein-air sketches (exh no. 6). Girtin seems to have revisited Devon in 1800 or 1801 (perhaps both years).[16] After touring Devon in the spring, Girtin no doubt went north later in the summer with a selection of Devon sketches.

In early autumn 1800 Girtin was back staying with a longstanding northern patron, David Erskine, 11th Earl of Buchan (1742-1829), at Dryburgh in Roxburghshire. For once, we have independent corroboration of this. Mary Ann's childhood friend and bridesmaid Miss Hog recalled meeting Girtin for the first time on the morning of his wedding, and he said that 'he had recently been in Scotland....at Melrose Abbey [and] the seat of Lord Buchan'.[17] Girtin married on 16th October 1800, at St George's Hanover Square, a stone's throw from Edward Lascelles's town house in Hanover Square. His bride was the sixteen-year-old Mary Ann Borrett, daughter of a wealthy Aldersgate Street goldsmith, Phineas Borrett. St George's was a fashionable Mayfair church with a rather racy reputation, and had regularised many irregular liaisons, including that of Sir William Hamilton and Emma Hart. According to one source, Girtin's was a 'runaway match' to which the bride's City merchant family – no doubt charmed by having a genius among it – quickly became indulgently reconciled.[18]

The friendship of Lord Buchan accounts for the important group of Girtin drawings made around Buchan's house at Dryburgh in the Scottish Borders: the abbeys of Melrose, Kelso and Dryburgh; the village and abbey of Jedburgh; and

6. ***An Estuary Scene, probably in Devon,*** *c.1801*
Harewood House Trust

The exact subject has not yet been identified but the watercolour has never left the Harewood Collection since it was bought by Edward Lascelles.

19. G&L 354 repr.
20. G&L 193, ex Sotheby's 14 July 1994 (103 repr.).
21. 'Anecdotes of Artists of the Last Fifty Years', *Library of the Fine Arts*, vol.iv, pp. 27-28. Turner demanded £400 a year and the right to keep some of the drawings; Elgin had to content himself with an Italian, Lusieri.
22. G&L 266ii.
23. Edward Lascelles' Collection, Inventory c.1814 (Leeds City Archives Department, Harewood Papers 520). Published in full in Hill 1995, pp. 57-58.
24. The painting was appreciatively noticed by the *Monthly Mirror* (June 1801, xi, p.376) and *The Porcupine* (28th April 1801).

the weirdly-shaped Eildon Hills which Girtin painted with austere beauty for Buchan in 1800. Unlike many of Girtin's patrons (the Longs, the Gowers, Lascelles) who were Tory supporters of Pitt, the Erskines were a committed Whig family, and probably more in tune with Girtin's own politics than most of his patrons. Buchan's brother Thomas Erskine, a friend of Fox and Sheridan, was the famous lawyer who resoundingly defended the 1794 Treason Trial Radicals, one of whom, Thomas Holcroft, later travelled with Girtin in Paris.

Buchan himself, the vain and eccentric founder of the Royal Society of Antiquaries of Scotland, had Romantic, antiquarian interests, with a particular passion for the history of his native land. He erected a statue to William Wallace on his Dryburgh estate, was a patron of Burns and Wordsworth and later inveigled Sir Walter Scott into being buried in the grounds of Dryburgh Abbey. Girtin's drawings of the soaring tracery of Melrose and the massive Norman ruin of Jedburgh touched Buchan's deepest interests. In turn, Girtin may have been encouraged by Buchan's literary sensibilities into a more overtly narrative Romanticism: a ghostly monk lurks in the russet shadows of a *c.*1798 watercolour of *Dryburgh Abbey.* [20]

By 1800, the year that he stayed with Buchan and once more at Harewood House, Girtin was spreading his wings – as Turner had done even earlier – beyond the confines of what was expected of a topographical watercolourist. In spring 1799 he had tetchily turned down the young Earl of Elgin's offer of a job as architectural draughtsman on Elgin's ambassadorial mission to Constantinople, on being offered only £30 a year, less than half the salary of 'his Lordship's valet de chambre', and being expected to help Lady Elgin decorate fire-screens.[21]

In 1799 Girtin seems to have been mobilising his northern patrons in support of his election as an Associate of the Royal Academy, though he had yet to qualify by exhibiting a painting in oils. Farington wrote on 9th February 1799: 'Mr Lascelles as well as Lady Sutherland are disposed to set up Girtin against Turner, – who they say effects his purpose by industry – the former more genius – Turner finishes too much'. Girtin's serious campaign to raise his professional profile was reflected in the six watercolours that he exhibited at the Royal Academy in April that year, which included the imposing (24 x 36 in), watercolour *Near Beddgelert.*[22] This was one of the finest watercolours owned by Edward Lascelles and had pride of place in the Large Drawing Room at Harewood House, Hanover Square.[23] In the event Turner, who had been exhibiting oils at the RA since 1796, was elected as an Associate. Girtin tried for election on 2nd November 1801, having exhibited a well-received oil of *Bolton Bridge* (now lost) at the RA in spring that year.[24] Surprisingly, he garnered not a single vote.

Probably in 1800, Girtin embarked upon an ambitious diversion from watercolours – he started to make sketches for a panorama of London as seen from near Blackfriars Bridge. This new type of public spectacle, invented by Robert Barker in 1788, could prove very lucrative – Girtin's friend Robert Ker Porter made no less than £1202 14s. 7½d. profit out of a panorama celebrating the British victory over Tippoo Sahib, *The Storming of Seringapatam,* in 1800-1.[25] Girtin's on-the-spot watercolour sketches in preparation for the panorama[26] far surpassed the lifeless precision of the Barker panoramas. The smoky complexity of his London views contrast with the monumental simplicity of Girtin's late northern landscapes, but are nonetheless among his most brilliant and innovative works.

In the summer of 1801 Girtin probably went to stay once more at Harewood, and also with another northern patron, Lord Mulgrave (1755-1831) at Mulgrave Castle near Whitby. Mulgrave was a soldier by profession, like his amiable bachelor brother the Hon. Edmund Phipps (1760-1837), another Girtin patron.[27] He was also Pitt's spokesman on military affairs, Foreign Secretary 1805-6 and a keen patron of the arts, with an early 18th century, fashionably-gothicised 'Castle', full of paintings by Rembrandt, Rubens, Claude and Titian. A Repton park enfolded the ruins of the original 13th century Mulgrave Castle, which Girtin sketched. Mulgrave may have got to know Girtin through Pitt's highly-placed, discreet political 'fixer', Charles Long, or through another Tory ally, Sir George Beaumont. (A few years after Girtin's death, Mulgrave and Beaumont launched the career of the young David Wilkie). The Longs were undoubtedly visitors to Mulgrave; Amelia Long, Girtin's talented favourite pupil, drew the rolling landscape looking towards Whitby[28] in a manner reminiscent of a pencil drawing by Girtin formerly known as 'Brough', but which has here been identified by David Hill as *Mulgrave Castle, looking towards Lythe* (see under exh no. 38).

Mulgrave, as he told Farington over dinner on 24th March 1807, had found Girtin 'a good-natured, open-dispositioned man', who had stayed with him 'when he laboured under the symptoms of an Asthma which not long afterwards killed him.' There was no falling off, however, in the quality of the drawings that derive from the Mulgrave tour. Lascelles owned the imposing upright drawing, dated 1801, of *Guisborough Priory* (exh. no. 39), a few miles from Mulgrave, possibly because his mother's family, the Chaloners, were from Guisborough. The slender ruin, seen side-on, soars with awesome beauty over the spectator, fragile yet enduring. The coastline around Mulgrave yielded such watercolours as *Sandsend,* 1802 (exh. no. 38), in which Girtin drew the rickety bridge over the inlet with a kind of playful, tensile calligraphy. There is also a broad sketch of nearby *Whitby*[29] with lowering clouds and light gleaming on the newly-washed sand, which strips the landscape to its essence.

25. Robert Ker Porter's Account Books, Seawright Collection, V&A.
26. G&L 225. Cf. V&A 1975 nos. 25-9.
27. A lost drawing of the *Coast of Sandsend,* 'presented by artist to Hon. E. Phipps, was in an anonymous sale at Christie's, 29th May 1873, lot 78. Cf. G&L p. 217.
28. Leeds City Art Gallery 797/39 (24a). Girtin's sketch of Mulgrave Castle is G&L 425, in The Shepherd sketch-book.
29. G&L 346 as Tynemouth, V&A 1975 no. 62 repr. Ex Sotheby's 13 November 1997 (44 repr.).
30. Mr Jackson quoted by Chambers Hall, whom Jenkins interviewed on 12th July 1852. RWS J 39/14.

31. Manuscript letter (Girtin's only substantial surviving letter) in the Whitworth Art Gallery, Manchester.
32. Wentworth Woodhouse mun. F34/198, Letters of Lady Harriet Cavendish, 50. Quoted in Sir Lewis Namier and John Brooke, *The History of Parliament: The House of Commons: 1790-1820,* Vol.4, pp 376-7, 1986, under Hon. Edward Lascelles.
33. Thomas Holcroft, *Travels from Hamburg to Paris,* 1804, pp. 488-498.

On 1st October 1801 the government agreed an Armistice with France and Girtin prevailed on his influential friends – both Mulgrave and Long later took the credit – to procure him a passport for Bonaparte's Paris, which all England was in agony to see after eight years of war. Leaving his eight-months'-pregnant wife at her father's house in Islington, he probably crossed to France about 1st November. Not, however, before an odd incident which throws light on Girtin's complex private life. Mr Jackson recounted how he had run into Girtin in a London street two days after he had apparently been seen off for the Dover packet. Girtin sheepishly asked him 'not to be angry. "he had only returned to take a farewell of a Lady whom he had forgotten to take leave of at the time of his departure".' Girtin stayed in Paris until late April or early May the following year.

There was probably some plan afoot to exhibit the London panorama in Paris and to prepare a Paris panorama for London, but Girtin wrote to his engraver brother John on 9th April 1802: 'I think the panorama here does not answer.' In the same letter he says: 'I altered my plan directly I got your letter for I had then Begun to sketch on a large scale and to Colour on the spot....But now I am for getting the Best Views I can and merly skeches'.[31] These were the panoramic, highly accurate but atmospheric pencil sketches which Girtin etched in softground on his return and which were aquatinted by various specialist printmakers as *Twenty Views of Paris* (1803).

The Paris sojourn must have been rather a dreary, lonely time for Girtin, though his spirit and humour flash through in little pencil caricatures of bombastic French officers, female fashion victims and pretty serving maids. The peace was fragile, the Parisians suspicious and Girtin, in time-honoured English custom, spoke no French. Like Hogarth before him, he was forced to sketch circumspectly, from hackney carriages, for fear of being arrested as a spy. Going so early to Paris, he probably missed the majority of the English who flooded there in the summer of 1802, once the Peace of Amiens had been securely signed on 27th March. They included the Opies, the Longs, and Edward Lascelles himself, who made quite an impact with his ever-open purse. As one Parisian quipped: 'Milord Henri Fitzgerald loue tout, Monsieur Greville dit mal de tout et Monsieur Lascelles achète tout'.[32]

Girtin did, however, run into that once-ardent Revolutionary, the playwright Thomas Holcroft, now long restored to respectability from his Treason Trials notoriety. Holcroft met Girtin complaining that he had 'no friend to accompany and aid him' and travelled with him for three days in the environs of Paris, during which Girtin sketched assiduously. He noted Girtin's uncannily assured style: 'His facility was great, and I was surprised at the dispatch with which he made his drawings'.[33] Girtin returned from Paris in late April or early May 1802 with these sketches and a handful of outstanding watercolours of Paris, including one of *Rue St Denis*[34] which is both a highly organised and a brilliantly complex evocation of urban architecture. The summer was busy with the softground etching of the *Twenty Views of Paris* and with the preparation for the exhibition of the London panorama or *Eidometropolis* (as it was grandly titled), which must have been painted before Girtin left for Paris. It opened on 2nd August 1802.[35]

The future must have seemed bright: Girtin had a crowd-catching London panorama, on view in Spring Gardens, not far from his painting room in the Strand; brand-new prints for a public anxious to see the First Consul's Paris, and he had supplied a backcloth design of the Conciergerie for Dibdin's pantomime at Drury Lane. It was not to be. On 25th October 1802 Sir George Beaumont wrote to Girtin from Cheltenham, anxious to obtain good impressions of the *Twenty Views of Paris.* He added, with real affection, 'you must take care of yourself'. [36] On 1st November, by the testimony of his brother John, Girtin was at work on his final watercolour, *St Anne's Gate, Salisbury*[37] – ghostly, unfinished, but painted with a consummate control of watercolour wash which rarely deserted him. He died on Lord Mayor's Day, 9th November 1802.

Although, when he died, Girtin's ground-breaking urban views were uppermost in the public mind – the panorama, reopened three days after his death for the benefit of his widow Mary Ann; and the Paris views, shrewdly marketed by his engraver brother – his northern landscapes remain among Girtin's supreme achievements. Girtin matured in the landscape of the north, profoundly influenced by its vast, open panoramas and dramatic weather; by the blocklike, rugged character of the northern vernacular architecture, which came to intrigue him, at the last, more than the showpiece medieval ruins which he had first sought there.

Girtin was lucky in his sympathetic circle of northern patrons, whose hospitality allowed him to feel at home in the landscape, away from the hurry of coach roads and uncomfortable inns that was the usual lot of the travelling artist. Just a few years later, the enlightened patronage of the Morritts at Rokeby Park encouraged a flowering of Cotman's genius; Turner found a haven in the congenial atmosphere of Walter Fawkes's Farnley, which had probably welcomed Girtin as well (see exh no. 30). Did Girtin have 'more genius' than Turner, as Lascelles's hasty judgement would have it? Of course not. But he certainly had a unique vision, which was emulated and exclaimed over, and which – because of his early death – retained the mystery of its promise. In the words of Turner, no better judge of a serious rival: he was truly 'a brilliant fellow'.

34. G&L 474ii, V&A 1975 no. 98 repr.
35. *Times* advertisement.
36. Jenkins's copy of the original letter 'in possession of [Girtin's] son', now lost. RWS J 39/19.
37. G&L 485. British Museum LB 46: 'dated and written under by his brother' according to Jenkins, who saw the drawing in the collection of Chambers Hall on 12th July 1852. The inscription, probably on an old mount, is now gone. RWS J 39/14.

Genius in the North

by David Hill

7. *John Hoppner*
Portrait of Edward Lascelles,
1797
Harewood House Trust

Edward Lascelles was one of the most fashionable beaux of his time, and one of the leading collectors of avant-garde art, including Girtin.

GIRTIN'S DEATH SEEMS to have come suddenly, if not without warning. When staying with Lord Mulgrave at Sandsend near Whitby, probably in the late spring of 1801, he was observed to be labouring under the symptoms of asthma.[1] On 27 June that year Edward Lascelles heard that Girtin was making plans to take a rest cure: 'I received your letter this morning and am sorry to hear that you are under the necessity of going to another climate for the benefit of your health'.[2] In the event he went to Paris. The following autumn he was again considering going abroad. On 25 October 1802 Sir George Beaumont wrote: 'The pleasure I feel at your successful labours is much allayed by the indifferent account you give of your health. You must take care of yourself, and I hope you will be enabled so to settle your concerns that you may pass the winter in Madeira. You will there find ample materials for your pencil, and the air is the most salubrious in the world'.[3] Just over a fortnight later he was dead. He died at his painting rooms-cum-lodgings over Norman's framemaker and printseller's shop in the Strand. His wife of only two years was with him. Outside crowds were gathering to watch the Lord Mayor's parade.[4]

The cause of death is uncertain. Asthma, as testified by Lord Mulgrave and others,[5] seems more likely than consumption as suggested by some accounts, and might well have been interpreted as 'ossification of the heart',[6] as it was described by one contemporary. Whatever the case, he hardly wasted away, still less took things easy. He married, set up home in St George's Row, overlooking Hyde Park, made several tours to visit his noble patrons, fathered a child, spent six months in Paris, painted and exhibited a colossal 1944 sq. foot circular panorama of London, worked on two drop-sets for the Covent Garden Theatre, painted a whole series of masterpieces in watercolour and produced a set of drawings and engravings of Paris. Far from easing off, one might suspect rather that Girtin worked himself to death.[7]

1. Farington Diary 24 March 1807.
2. Roget i110. Jenkins's copy of the letter, 'the original in the possession of [Girtin's] son', is Jenkins MSS RWS J 39/19.
3. Roget i113. Jenkins's copy of the original letter 'in possession of [Girtin's] son', now lost. RWS J 39/19.
4. Roget i113. The information that theses rooms were his lodgings comes from E. Edwards, *Anecdotes of Painting,* 1808, pp.279-280, quoted G&L 116.
5. Including his obituarist in the *Gentleman's Magazine,* February 1803 p.187 repr Mayne p.77.
6. Cited by Roget i110.
7. Perhaps literally. It is striking that the reports of his asthma occur from 1801, when he would have been working on his panorama. This kind of activity, and scene painting, could quite easily have caused serious complications. It is noteworthy that Dayes (below) says that he originally had a vigorous constitution.

The funeral was held on 17 November 1802 at St Paul's Church, Covent Garden. Apart from his family, there was also present a number of patrons including Sir William Beechey and Sir George Beaumont, and friends from the artistic community including Thomas Hearne, Henry Edridge and Turner,[8] the last just returned from a tour to the Alps and a period of study in Paris.[9] It was the same church in which Turner had been baptised, and the following year Turner paid for a memorial stone inscribed "Sacred to the memory of Thomas Girtin, Artist, who departed this life Nov. the 9th, 1802, aged 27 years'.[10] Turner reflected: "We were friends to the last, though *they* did what they could to separate us",[11] and reviewed his friend's talents trenchantly: "If Tom Girtin had lived, I should have starved".[12]

Turner could afford to be generous. In 1802 he had been elected a full member of the Royal Academy. By contrast Girtin's career seems to have run backwards. From setting himself and his young bride up in grand style in 1800, by the end of the following year he was borrowing money from his brother so that he could fund his trip to Paris,[13] and abandoning his wife to live with her parents in Islington where she was to bear their son alone. Even in those days this must have seemed a somewhat less than optimal way to begin married life, and one might surmise that these circumstances were forced rather than chosen. In the autumn of 1801 he seems to been in an uncommon hurry to set out for Paris. The opportunity to travel through the Peace of Amiens had barely been announced when Girtin's high-ranking noble patrons were pulling strings to procure him an early passport.[14] In the end he was forced to admit that the panorama of London on which he had been working, and into which he had no doubt sunk a considerable investment, 'does not answer'.[15] He returned to London with little to show for a stay of six months except some fine sketches of the city and its environs. He managed to show the panorama in London during the summer of 1802, but by then most of his audience was away enjoying Paris. Sir George Beaumont's letter of 27 October 1802 hints that all was not well with Girtin's finances: 'I hope you will be enabled so to *settle your concerns* [my italics] that you may pass the winter in Madeira". According to his wife Mary Anne, Girtin had got quite used to the grand life. He was, she said: 'too fond of refined society to enjoy that of the illiterate and vulgar. He lived so much with his superiors in rank and station that it gave him a distaste of the middle classes.'[16] Perhaps there is more than a hint in this that he had been living beyond his means. To end up living above a shop must have seemed to him akin to having fallen from heaven. "Poor Tom", Turner was wont to reflect.[17]

Even if his domestic circumstances faltered, the quality of Girtin's work forged ahead, and whatever his troubles, they were most decidedly not a product of the quantity or quality of his work. During the

8. Roget i113.
9. Cf. D Hill, *Turner in the Alps,* 1993.
10. Roget i113. The stone had disappeared by the end of the 19th century. Some new memorial would seem required.
11. A J Finberg, *Life of J M W Turner,* 1961, p.92.
12. W Thornbury, *Life and Correspondence of J M W Turner,* 1877 p.71.
13. Roget i111.
14. Cf. G&L p.43 n.4, citing Roget i110.
15. Letter to John Girtin from Paris, 9 March 1802 (Whitworth Art Gallery, Manchester). Quite what he meant by 'does not answer' is unclear, but it would appear that he went to Paris with the intention of showing his panorama. It would seem that he could not raise any interest.
16. Roget i115.
17. W Cosmo Monkhouse, *Turner,* 1879, p.24

18. W Redgrave, *Century of Painters,* i 390-3, quoted in Roget i89
19. Cf. Roget i95
20. Published posthumously in *The Works of the Late Edward Dayes,* 1805, p.329
21. Roget i116
22. Miss Mary Hogg, the best friend of Girtin's wife, Mary Ann Borrett, confessed to having been in love with him cf. G&L p.111
23. W H Pyne, *Somerset House Gazette,* 1824 p. 82 quoted G&L p.110.

last two years he painted a string of masterpieces. It is noteworthy how many of these are north of England subjects. As one of his first biographers put it: 'Inspired by the dark and true and tender north, he began to treat mountain and lake scenery in a manner very different from his predecessors, imitating the effects of heavy overhanging clouds throwing the vast mass of mountain which occupied the whole distance under a deep and solemn mass of gloom'.[18] For Girtin as with Turner, the 'rough-hewn matter' of the north of England opened up to him the poetry of the sublime. But whereas for Turner it was revealed in dramatic circumstances, for Girtin the sublime manifested itself more in quiet corners, and expressed itself in a sense of transcendent quiet. It is almost irresistible to see his achievement of such moments as the projection in some way of his physical condition: the necessity of finding health through contact with nature, and the attainment of tranquillity and grace in that contact. In the event it could be that contact which caused his demise, for he was wont to paint out of doors in all weathers, and at least one contemporary thought that he must have died from catching a chill.[19]

We have already heard that his apprenticeship with Edward Dayes was not entirely to the employer's satisfaction. Nevertheless there is something rather darker suggested by the short biographical note that Dayes penned the year after Girtin's death:[20]

GIRTIN THOMAS – LANDSCAPE

This artist died November the 9th, 1802, after a long illness, in the twenty-eighth year of his age. Biography is useful to stimulate to acts of industry and virtue; or, by exhibiting the contrary, to enable us to shun the fatal consequences of vice. While our heart bleeds at the premature death of the subject of this paper, it becomes equally an act of justice to caution young persons against the fatal effects of suffering their passions to overpower their reason, and to hurry them into acts of excess, that may, in the end, render life a burthen, destroy existence, or bring on a premature old age. Though his drawings are generally too slight, yet they must ever be admired as the offspring of a strong imagination. Had he not trifled away a vigorous constitution, he might have arrived at a very high degree of excellence as a landscape painter.

This is enough to make one's curiosity boggle. Nor can it be dismissed as simply the bile of yesterday's man, outmoded by his pupil. Dayes states clearly that something terrible happened to Girtin's reputation, fortune and health. There may be several things here, living above his station, his 'great carelessness in money matters,[21] or allowing his attractiveness to the ladies get the better of him,[22] or worse, 'continued sensual indulgence' that 'enfeebled his mental powers'.[23] We can only wonder, but we can infer that Dayes knew all too well of these events and lamented them for his young protégé's sake. In the light of this,

Girtin's frequent choice of simple subjects in the north of England might very well have seemed to offer him a solid alternative to the shifting sands of his metropolitan life.

His contact with the north was encouraged by a network of north country patrons including Sir John Ramsden of Byram Park near Ferrybridge, Miss Winn of Nostell Priory near Wakefield, George Selby of Twizzell near Bamburgh in Northumberland, Lord Buchan of Dryburgh Abbey in the Scottish borders, Walter Fawkes of Farnley Hall near Otley, Sir William Pilkington of Chevet Hall near Wakefield and Lord Mulgrave of Mulgrave Park near Whitby.[24] Primarily, however, it is Edward Lascelles (cf. exh. no. 7), eldest son of the first Earl of Harewood, who accounts for Girtin's repeated visits to the north, and who encouraged his work through to its maturity. He was an equally generous early supporter of Turner, inviting him to Harewood in 1797 and thus providing a springboard for Turner's formative tour of the north in that year.[25] Nevertheless Lascelles's relationship with Girtin was the closer. He bought a larger number of works, nineteen in total against eleven by Turner in the same period. Girtin returned to Harewood so frequently that it is said that a room was kept permanently ready for his use.[26] Lascelles paid Girtin for lessons. An album of drawings by Lascelles survives in the library at Harewood, and it is possible that watercolours such as *Temple in Harewood Park* (exh. no. 8) or *Ships in a Harbour* (exh no. 9) were made in the context of this instruction. In 1800 Girtin assisted Lord Harewood with some visualisations of the effects of Humphrey Repton's proposed developments to the landscape of the park at Harewood.[27] Great as was his admiration for Turner, Edward Lascelles was nevertheless one of those tempted to pit one against the other. On 9 February 1799 when Turner was lobbying for support in the forthcoming elections for associates of the Royal Academy Farington recorded that 'Mr Lascelles as well as Lady Sutherland are disposed to

8. ***Temple in Harewood Park***, *c.1798*
Yale Center for British Art, Paul Mellon Collection

Possibly recording a now-disappeared temple at Harewood.

24. These are dealt with in more detail by Susan Morris above. Sir William Pilkington was also a collector of Turner, a friend of Walter Fawkes of Farnley Hall, and owned at least one large watercolour by Girtin, Bolton Abbey, G&L 438 repr.
25. Cf. Hill 1996.
26. Roget i96.
27. Borenius 1936 p. vi, n.1, cited in Hill 1995, p..61 n.59.

28. G&L p.29, where dated impossibly to 1798.
29. Cf. Hill 1996 p.152 ff.
30. Leeds City Archives Department, Personal Account books of Edward Lascelles, Junior, (189).
31. Roget i120.
32. Account-books 189 and 191.
33. Roget i120.
34. G&L 271 repr, where dated to 1798, V&A P129 1920.
35. G&L 436 as 'Harewood Castle and Park', V&A 1975 no. 85 repr.

set up Girtin against Turner who they say effects his purposes by industry – the former more genius – Turner finishes too much'.

It was the scenery of the north of England that first liberated that genius. Following his tour of 1796, over the succeeding winter Girtin worked up no fewer that ten watercolours for exhibition at the Academy in 1797. It was the greatest number that he was to show together in his life, and must have been intended to mark his debut as a fully-independent artist with a flourish. The critics seem not to have paid very much attention, but it is unlikely that his fellow-artists were so blind. The most perceptive of eyes, those of Turner, seem to have been positively dazzled. Although Turner had travelled a little already, the sheer ambition and scope of Girtin's undertaking, and the sublimity of the places he had visited, must have struck him with the force of a revelation. Within weeks of the exhibition opening, Turner was on the road to the north himself. He visited nearly every one of Girtin's sites, and we can be certain that he must have quizzed Girtin for hints and information to the full extent that their friendship allowed.

9. ***Ships in a Harbour,*** *c.1798*
Harewood House Trust

Possibly made while giving lessons to Edward Lascelles. The detail of figures caulking the side of the ship brings the whole composition to life in a manner typical of Girtin.

10. ***Ships in a Harbour,*** *c.1798*
Harewood House Trust

The pencil sketch on which the watercolour was based. Only rediscovered in 1997.

Turner had already secured the patronage of Edward Lascelles and he visited Harewood on his tour. There is no indication that Girtin did so in 1796 but a tradition has it that the two friends sketched together in the park at Harewood.[28] Turner's only visit was in 1797 and while we have ample evidence of his work at that time,[29] there is nothing by Girtin that could be dated with any certainty to such a visit. Nevertheless Lascelles' payments to Turner for work dating from his 1797 visit are dated 21 November 1797 and 15 March 1798, while the first payment to Girtin is dated 17 February 1798.[30] The latter is presumably for work that had been conceived the previous summer, and taken together these payments might suggest that the tradition could be more than just wishful thinking.

The payment to Girtin on 17 February 1798 was of five guineas 'for a drawing'. This must have been quite a substantial item, for we know that the previous year he sold one of his Royal Academy exhibits, a watercolour of *Jedburgh Abbey* measuring 19 by 27 inches, for six guineas.[31] Further payments followed: £20.0.0 on 9 May 1798, for two, or possibly three items; £17.17.0 on 21 November 1798 'for Drawings, lessons, &c'; £33.12.0 on 15 July 1799 'for Drawings'; £20.0.0 on 15 January 1800 'for two drawings'; and £32.12.0 on 17 February 1801 'for several drawings'.[32] The last-known transaction is recorded in a letter to Girtin from Edward Lascelles dated 27 July 1801 in which he made arrangements for the payment of 80 guineas for some 'Drawings of this place', to which he had asked that certain alterations be made.[33] Only the last payment can be confidently identified with specific pictures. The reference to 'drawings of this place' must include the two large watercolours of *Harewood House from the South East* and *Harewood House from the South West,* both still at Harewood (exh nos.1 and 11) plus the similarly-sized watercolours of *Plompton Rocks* in the Victoria and Albert Museum[34] and *Knaresborough* at the Whitworth Art Gallery, Manchester, which is dated 1801.[35]

11. ***Harewood House from the South West,*** *1801*
Harewood House Trust

The house is only just visible over the trees. Instead Girtin commentates on the wide variety of late-summer agricultural activity that he has discovered on the estate.

*12. **Harewood House from the South East**, c.1797*
Yale Center for British Art, Paul Mellon Collection

The concentration and sensitivity of detail suggests that this must date from Girtin's first visit to Harewood. Later sketches tend to be much broader.

As for the rest we may only guess, but we can reconstruct the collection with reasonable certainty from an inventory of *c.*1814[36] and a sale catalogue of 1858.[37] The large watercolour of *Guisborough Priory* is dated 1801 (exh no. 39) and must therefore be one of the 'several' drawings paid for on 17 February 1801. Another candidate for this group would be *Lodore Falls* (exh no. 13), since Lascelles would have been interested in this subject having made a tour to the Lake District in 1800 (see under no. 36). Another member of this group might have been *Village at the Bend of a River* now at Toledo in the USA.[38] The payment of twenty pounds on 15 January 1800 might well have included *Ilkley* (exh no. 20) and *Harewood Bridge* (exh no. 22), which would date them to the summer of 1799. The payment of thirty-two guineas on 15 July 1799 would almost certainly have included two large watercolours of *Snowdon* and *Bethgellert,* which are known to have been in the collection[39] and which themselves must be identifiable with two Bethgellert subjects which Girtin exhibited at the Royal Academy that year.[40] Payments of 21 November 9 May and 17 February 1798 would probably have included, *The Rocking Stone*[41] and *Ships in a Harbour* (exh no. 9) and *On the Wharfe* (exh no. 19).

Apart from the tour of 1796 there is little evidence to date Girtin's visits to Harewood and other sites in the north. From the tradition that a room was kept ready for his use, and from the regularity of Edward Lascelles' payments, we can infer that he was a regular visitor. Despite the fact that he made a tour to the west country in 1797, a visit to Yorkshire at some stage in that year seems possible, not only on account of the first payment to him occurring in the following spring, but also because in 1798 Girtin exhibited two watercolours of *Rievaulx Abbey* at the Royal Academy.[42] Rievaulx lies in the foothills of the north Yorkshire moors and would have been somewhat out of the line of sites that we know him to have visited in 1796. It actually places him nearer to Lord Mulgrave at Whitby than to Edward Lascelles at Harewood. It is possible that a fine pencil drawing of *Harewood House from the South East* (exh no. 12) dates from this time. It is in a much more careful manner than the sketches of around 1800, and so diligent as to suggest that it must have been made on Girtin's first

36. Published in full in Hill 1995 p.57-8.
37. Christie's 1 May 1858. Cf. Hill 1995 p. 51.
38. G&L 380, sometime known as 'Bethgellert' and 'In the grounds of Harewood Park'. There is a less refined version in the British Museum, 1948-210-9-5.

visit to the house. Any visit in 1798 would have been squeezed in around a known tour of north Wales in that year, but 1799 seems possible, and we know that he was at Harewood and Northumberland in 1800. A sketch of Harewood House in the Shepherd sketchbook is dated to that year (Fig. III), and as we have already heard, he returned from Dryburgh shortly before his marriage in October.[43] It seems very likely that he was very busy in the north in 1800, for we know him to have made tours of the Craven Dales and to the Lakes about this time, and this might well have been in the company of Edward Lascelles who made a tour to these regions in the summer (see under exh no. 36). One product of Girtin's visit to the Lakes was the large watercolour of *Lodore Falls* (exh. no. 13), which was bought by Lascelles. His final journey to the north seems to have been in the spring of 1801 when he visited Mulgrave Castle and Northumberland. Given that he spent part of the following months working on four Yorkshire subjects for Edward Lascelles, it seems highly likely that this was also his last visit to Harewood. In all we can count nearly three hundred works by Girtin of north of England and Scottish border subjects. This is over half of his entire output.[44] He must have seemed to reek of the northern hills.

The genius of the north produced effects that were not entirely to everyone's taste. One of the watercolours of *Rievaulx Abbey* that Girtin exhibited at the Academy in 1798[45] brought forth such vituperation from the *Whitehall Evening Post* on 2 June as to make one suspect that the writer must have been in cahoots with Edward Dayes:

> *We should have passed over the extreme slovenliness of this drawing, if we had not recognised the same fault in all this artist's performances. From the wildness which pervades them, it may be fairly presumed that they have been done in a hurry, which is at the best but a sorry apology for neglect and carelessness. We enlarge upon this topic, as it is evident Mr Girtin can produce better works if he pleases. We would recommend to his serious consideration the excellent maxim of Lord Chesterfield, "Whatever is worth doing, is worth doing well." The present article is drawn with considerable spirit and ability which such scenes indispensably require.*[46]

Fig. III
***Harewood House from the South West,** 1800*
Shepherd sketchbook, The Whitworth Art Gallery, University of Manchester

A page from the one surviving book of Girtin drawings.

From previous page

39. Cf. Christie's 1 May 1858 (21) 'A grand view of Snowdon with clouds hanging at the foot of the Mountain, a river in the foreground' and (44) 'Bethgellaert. A very fine work.' The former was bought by C S Bale for 45 guineas (the highest price for any of the Girtins) and is identifiable with G&L 266ii. The second was bought by Palser for £15.4..6 but is unidentified with any work known at present. However, a watercolour sketch of Bedgellert in the Shepherd sketchbook (Hardie 1939 no.4, G&L 361, records the composition of an untraced watercolour which was engraved by S W Reynolds as 'Beddgelert' and published on 7 May 1824 (cf. Mayne p. 55 and 91).
40. RA 1799 347/381 Bethkellert, North Wales.
41. G&L 288, V&A 1975 no.48 repr, Tate Gallery, London, 4409
42. RA 1798 nos. 493, 650
43. A pencil sketch of *Dunstanburgh from the North* at the Yale Center for British Art (B1975.3.1179), G&L 162; Morris 1986, no.44, is normally dated c.1796, but its breadth of handling and panoramic feel suggests a date more of 1800 or 1801. There are splashes of watercolour on the reverse indicating perhaps the existence of an untraced watercolour.

'Spirit' and even 'wildness' were clearly qualities which Girtin intended to communicate. The more discriminating among his audience, however, could perceive this to be a virtue. Commenting on the same exhibition the critic of the *Monthly Mirror* observed: 'Girtin's productions... though not so softened as Turner's... display so much daring and vigorous execution, that a sedulous attention to the finishing would perhaps be injurious to the effect'.[47] It was precisely Girtin's economy which Lascelles admired when he contrasted Girtin's exercise of genius with Turner's reliance on industry.

Girtin's work must nevertheless have seemed discordantly rough-hewn in the ormolu world of late Georgian Britain. In this context his watercolours must have seemed no more than stained scraps. This was, however, obviously an effect at which Girtin connived. He deliberately chose a coarse-looking paper, a prominently wire-marked cartridge flecked with the detritus of the recycled linen rags from which it was made. Such was the importance of this paper to his artistic purpose that only one particular sort would do: 'The paper which he most admired was only to be had of a stationer at Charing Cross; this was cartridge, with slight wire marks, and folded like foolscap or post. It commonly happened that the part which had been folded, when put on the stretching frame would sink into spots in a line, entirely across the centre of the sky; so that where the crease had been, the colour was so many degrees of a darker hue than the general tone of the sky. This unsightly accident was not only overlooked, but in some instances really admired, inasmuch, that it was taken for a sign of originality, and in the transfer of his drawings from one collector to another, bore a premium, according to that indubitable mark...'.[48] The paper not only had a coarse texture, but also particular qualities of absorption, which enabled him to work his colours very wet: 'His colour settled without hard edges; his second wash was absorbed without bringing the under colour away. There was not, and could not be, any rubbing or scrubbing, or anything but the slightest alteration in his work; the material demanded, and obtained, directness'.[49] Turner by contrast normally used a tough Whatman paper which allowed him to work out his colour much further, and to overwash, soak, scratch, abrade and recolour to an unprecedentedly high-wrought and complex degree of finish.[50] Girtin went quite the other way. His purpose was to preserve spontaneous effects, the very autograph of his spirit, and in such a direct manner as to require of him the utmost clarity of utterance: 'his method of work', as one contemporary described it, 'was careful, notwithstanding his bold execution, even to fastidiousness'.[51] The result was a simplified breadth of application that seems to apprehend the very essence of things.

We are particularly fortunate to have a detailed description by a contemporary painter, W.H.Pyne, of the exact procedures and colours used by Girtin.

We know, therefore, that he used ultramarine, prussian blue, indigo, yellow lake, gamboge, Roman ochre, cologne-earth, madder brown, burnt sienna, Vandyck brown, brown pink, and light, Venetian and Indian reds. With a little translation into modern equivalents, this might be used as a recipe for repeating Girtin's effects today, and would certainly serve as a useful tool for understanding the way in which his pictures were built up. It is striking, however, to realise just how unfortunately central to his process were fugitive colours. Lakes figure all too prominently, and indigo, just about the most notorious of all colours in respect of fading, was mixed with almost everything, and particularly with indian red, light red and lake, to give luminosity to his skies Indigo in its fresh state is a violet-blue which would have given a slatey appearance to his greys. It has faded from almost every example in the present exhibition, with the notable exception of *The Abbey Mill* (exh no. 27).

It would be a mistake, however, to assume that Girtin's watercolours were ever much more colourful as such. In fact the freshest examples are if anything all the more reticent. The brighter primaries are usually well-preserved, but used in extremely restricted touches. Girtin's colour would rarely have been strident but would rather have had more contrast, the lights have been brighter, and the compositions more instinct with the freshness of air and space. Rather than opulence of colour and paint, Girtin relied on judicious choice, sparing application and intelligence of concept and design. As a result of time the latter has come to appear even more decisive than originally. Every example in the present exhibition has interest with respect to its design. Suffice it to mention but a few in this introduction: The position of the main motif – the bridge – in *Harewood Bridge* (exh no. 22) and the *Ouse Bridge, York* (exh no. 32), boldly confined to one half of the composition only; the sense of space in *Kirkstall Abbey* (exh no. 15) achieved by leading the eye constantly to, and beyond, the edges of the composition; the way in which *Stepping Stones on the Wharfe* (exh no. 18) is constructed around a line of light which cuts the whole composition diagonally in half, or the fact that *On the Wharfe* (exh no. 19) confronts us with a blank bluff of material which is relieved only by a glimpse of the sky at the top left, and is broken only by the vertical accent of the standing shepherd. Few, if any, of his compositions rely on the conventional devices of Claude Lorrain as did Turner's, and equally few make use of a conventional *repoussoir* in the foreground, again as Turner usually did, to give the compositions depth. Some of Girtin's compositional devices, such as the exaggeratedly off-centre placement of the house in *Harewood House from the South East* (exh no. 1) seem to have been designed to raise eyebrows. He positively sought out unusual subjects, or oblique approaches to popular ones. So keen was he to avoid

44. G&L list a total output of just over 500 items.
45. Perhaps that now at the V&A, London, (FA 499) G&L 250.
46. Quoted Mayne p.46.
47. Quoted G&L p.115.
48. W H Pyne, *Somerset House Gazette*, 1824, quoted Hardie 1934, p.8.
49. Hardie, 1934, p.9.
50. Cf. P Bower, Turner's Papers, Tate Gallery, 1990.
51. *Library of Fine Arts*, 1832, iii 318, quoted in G&L p.110, n.4.
52. W H Pyne, *Somerset House Gazette*, 1824, quoted Hardie, 1834, pp. 8-9

53. Roget i120.
54. Farington *Diary,* 24 March 1807.
55. Roget i116
56. C R Leslie, *Handbook for Young Painters,* London 1855, p.266, quoted G&L p.95

the conventional preoccupations of artists that his details of the house in *Harewood House from the South East* are inaccurate. Edward Lascelles even wrote to ask for the details to be altered.[53] There are no signs of Girtin having complied.

Finally it is salutary to wonder that Edward Lascelles admired Girtin at all. Lascelles was the eldest son of one of the richest men in all England. Educated, urbane, a flamboyant Regency beau who could afford any indulgence that life could offer. Why should he have found a rope-maker's son and his works of the least interest, still less as imbued with a quality which he would describe as genius? We may sense something from looking at Girtin's portrait by John Opie (exh no. 2). Wide-eyed and animated, the artist is projected as unfeignedly enthusiastic and honest. Lord Mulgrave was impressed with his 'open-dispositioned nature',[54] and from other sources we hear of his 'generous and giddy' character.[55] Even Dayes speaks of his passions, his imagination and his vigour. Coupled with the unrefined vestiges of his tradesman-class origins, his good looks, evident magnetism especially to young women, dashing 'sword-play of his pencil',[56] and his devotion to landscape, particularly that of the north, he must have seemed the very personification of the natural, a breath of air wafting through the confines of drawing-room life. The fact that he was forced to gasp for this air, and then had it snatched from him while still young makes the sense of it in his work all the more vivid and valuable.

BIBLIOGRAPHY AND ABBREVIATIONS

Borenius T Borenius, *Catalogue of the Pictures and Drawings at Harewood House,* 1936

Davies R Davies, *Thomas Girtin's Watercolours,* London 1922

G&L T Girtin and D Loshak, *The Art of Thomas Girtin,* London 1954

Hardie 1934 M Hardie, 'Thomas Girtin: The Technical Aspect of his Work', in *Journal of the Old Watercolour Society,* XI, 1934, pp. 1-20

Hardie 1939 M Hardie *'A sketchbook of Thomas Girtin',* in Walpole Society, XXVII, 1939, pp. 89-95

Hill 1995 D Hill, *Harewood Masterpieces: English Watercolours and Drawings,* Harewood, 1995

Hill 1996 D Hill, *Turner in the North,* Yale University Press, London, 1996

Jenkins Manuscript notes of John Joseph Jenkins (1811-1885), in the archives of the Royal Watercolour Society, Bankside, London.

Mayne J Mayne, *Thomas Girtin,* Leigh on Sea, 1949

Morris 1986 S Morris, *Thomas Girtin,* catalogue of the exhibition at the Yale Center for British Art, New Haven, USA, 1986

Morris 1996 S Morris, 'Girtin, Thomas', entry in the *Macmillan Encyclopaedia of Art,* 1996

Roget J L Roget, *History of the Old Watercolour Society,* two volumes, 1891

V&A 1975 F Hawcroft, *Watercolours by Thomas Girtin,* catalogue of the exhibition at the Whitworth Art Gallery Manchester and the Victoria and Albert Museum, London, 1975

Girtin's Northern Excursions

by David Hill

Girtin used Harewood as a base from which to visit a wide range of sites in the north. The following section looks at a selection of these in detail. The numbering sequence continues that of the illustrations in the introductory sections of this catalogue, and corresponds to that of the exhibition list on pp. 63-4.

13. ***Lodore Falls, Derwentwater,*** *c.1800*
The Visitors of the Ashmolean Museum, Oxford

Edward Lascelles made a tour to the Lakes in 1800. It is possible that Girtin might have accompanied him. In any case this became one of the core pieces of the Lascelles collection.

14. *Kirkstall Abbey with a canal barge, evening, 1802*

Private Collection, courtesy of Agnew's, London

Kirkstall Abbey stands about three miles east of Leeds city centre. It was well-known in the later eighteenth century and appealed both to antiquarian and romantic taste.[1] During the period of his apprenticeship to Edward Dayes, probably *c.*1794, Girtin painted two watercolours[2] for James Moore his antiquarian patron, and was thus familiar with the site before any visit. We might therefore have expected him to have made Kirkstall an important site on his first tour of the north in 1796 but thus far no evidence of such a visit has yet come to light. It seems not to have been until the later years of his association with Harewood that he made a visit at all. Turner had made it a major subject on his tour of 1797[3] and produced one substantial watercolour to exhibit at the Royal Academy in 1798[4] and another to sell in the same year to Edward Lascelles.[5] Turner's example seems to have spurred Girtin's interest for in 1800 he made a watercolour of the view of *Kirkstall Abbey from Kirkstall Hill*[6] from exactly the same viewpoint as one of Turner's sketches.[7] This was accompanied by a watercolour of Kirkstall village,[8] and followed in the last years of his life by the two watercolours exhibited here.

Kirkstall Abbey with a canal barge, evening, records the view, now largely obscured by trees, from the Leeds/Liverpool canal at the foot of Kirkstall Forge Locks, about half a mile south west of the abbey ruins. A barge has tied up for the night and its team of horses is being led away to be watered and fed. Sunlight rakes the ruins from the north west. The composition is based on a pencil sketch now at the Yale Center for British Art.[9] The sketch is similar in size and style to other Yorkshire subjects in the Shepherd sketchbook at the Whitworth Art Gallery, Manchester. A number of watercolours in this exhibition are derived from drawings in the sketch-book which must be dateable to 1800 or 1801. Like the finished watercolour these drawings are also characterised by a reductive and direct monumentality. If the signature and date is correct, the present watercolour must have been made in the last months of Girtin's life following his return to London from Paris in May 1802.

1. Cf. William Bishop, 'Views of Kirkstall Abbey', *Leeds Arts Calendar,* no. 81, 1977 p.10 ff.
2. Ashmolean Museum, Oxford DBB 698 (G&L 20i) and Yale Center for British Art, New Haven, USA, B1975.3.1141, (G&L 19). Girtin and Loshak date both of these c.1792, but this seems to me to be too early. Both are extremely competent productions, and a date of c.1794 seems more appropriate. The latter is related to a pencil drawing in the Turner Bequest at the Tate Gallery, possibly by Dayes, TB CCCLXXVII 18
3. Cf.Hill 1996, p.22 ff.
4. Sir John Soane's Museum, London (Hill 1996 p.23 repr. colour)
5. Fitzwilliam Museum, Cambridge (Hill 1996 p.29 repr. colour)
6. British Museum 1855-2-14-53. Unfortunately not made available to this exhibition, but repr. Hill 1996 p.27 colour, with a photograph of the view today.
7. Turner Bequest, Tate Gallery, TB XXXIV 15 repr b/w Hill 1996 p.27
8. If the traditional identification is correct (G&L 449)
9. Yale Center for British Art, New Haven, USA, B1975.3.1027.

10. This watercolour has hitherto been wrongly titled *Kirkstall Abbey, Evening.*
11. Quoted in Bishop op cit p.13
12. Roget, i91.

15. *Kirkstall Abbey from the bridge, morning, c.1802*

The Victoria and Albert Museum, London

Indisputably one of Girtin's masterpieces. Recording the view from Kirkstall bridge with the river Aire in the foreground, looking north to the abbey ruins, the scene is perfectly recognisable today. In the watercolour low sunlight slants in from the east[10] and gleams beneath dark skies. The present watercolour might almost be considered as a pendant to *Kirkstall Abbey with a canal barge, evening,* contrasting morning with evening, the river with the canal, and dark skies with light. The cattle remain seated in the meadow portending rain. The abbey ruins are smothered with vegetation. We might surmise that the sunlit foreground and meadow was originally rather brighter against the shaded ruins, but the sense of light lancing into darkness is still powerfully present, played out on a typically essential structure. In such stillness the consciousness of movement is made all the more apparent. Birds cawing around the tower, figures walking in the field, a small dog scampering to the gate.

Fig. IV
Kirkstall Abbey from the Bridge
(Photograph: David Hill)

Exactly the same view was described in 1827 by the anonymous author of the *Historical Account of Kirkstall Abbey:* After a few paces farther... unexpectedly bursts on the sight the tranquil and pensive beauty of the desolate monastery, as it reposes in the lap of pastoral luxurience... from the Inn at Kirkstall Bridge, the whole range before the eye presents an aspect of rural quiet and grandeur blended with traits of a deep but tender melancholy'.[11] The writer might well have been brought to this spot and taught these feelings by sight of Girtin's composition, which was engraved by W B Cooke for his *River Scenery by Turner and Girtin,* and published in 1824.

The matter of time of day would have been a fundamental concern to an artist such as Girtin. In the process of colouring which he learned from Dayes the first stage was to decide on the angle of light so that one might then lay in any areas of shade, cast shadows &c in neutral tone, before applying washes of colour. This was a process which he was to depart from in many of his more mature works, but the habit of considering the light never left him. He implemented this in his teaching: 'he would point out the time of day, the cast shadows and particular effect suited to the time and scene &c – a mode of teaching far in advance of the time'.[12]

13. Farington Diary, 14 November 1795.
14. At the Whitworth Art Gallery, Manchester, cf. Hardie 1939, (G&L 376 i, 375 and 377).
15. G&L 378i sold Sotheby's 14 March 1962 lot 69, G&L 391 now Yale Center for British Art, New Haven, USA, and G&L 441i, exhibited here as No. 17.
16. G&L 378ii sold Sotheby's 12 March 1987 lot 62; G&L 367iii Eton College collection, G&L 376iv N.M.Wales, Cardiff, and G&L 438 Private Collection. Another watercolour (G&L 440) comprehensively reinvents the architecture of Bolton. It would seem that its maker either did not understand the actual architecture of the site or at least had no concern to represent it.
17. G&L p.119.

Fig. VI
Bolton Abbey East End from across the River Wharfe
(Shepherd sketchbook, The Whitworth Art Gallery, University of Manchester)

*16. **Bolton Abbey, the east end from across the river Wharfe**, 1800*

Leeds Museums and Galleries (City Art Gallery)

The view looking across the river Wharfe to the great east window and north transept. Late morning sun from the left. A muscular tonal effect, although faded.

Bolton Priory, as it should be called, remains today one of the most beautifully situated monastic sites in Britain. By Girtin's time it was becoming increasingly well-known as a picturesque site. Edward Lascelles went there in 1795 with the portrait painter John Hoppner who found it remarkable and also reported: 'Young Mr Lascelles... has a taste for the arts, & has practiced a little'.[13] In the light of this it is surprising, as at Kirkstall, that nothing survives to demonstrate a visit by Girtin on his first tour to the north of 1796. As at Kirkstall he seems not to have made the excursion until the later years of his association with Harewood.

A clutch of sketches survives to us, three in the Shepherd sketchbook[14] and three others probably made on the same visit.[15] Assuming the accuracy of the date inscribed on the present watercolour, we might surmise that the visit occurred in that year. Apart from the watercolours exhibited here, another four were made from these same sketches.[16]

Girtin's approach to the site and his selection of viewpoints demonstrates at the least a certain independence of mind. At the extreme it might evidence a degree of idiosyncrasy and obliquity that deserves calling genius. Most other visitors approached direct by road or riverside footpath on the same (right) bank on which the ruins are situated. Girtin chose the opposite side by crossing Bolton bridge and approached on the left bank. His situation on the opposite bank had the very great virtue of enabling him easily to bring the river into the foreground of his composition as in the present example. Whilst there he must at least have surveyed the prospect of crossing the stepping stones, back to the priory, since they appear in the foreground of his sketch (fig. IV). The fact that they were omitted from the finished watercolour might also suggest that on this occasion discretion proved the better part of valour.

The main idea in his selection of viewpoint seems to have been to record the way in which trees were springing up all around the ruins. He considerably developed this effect in the finished watercolour, to the extent that the trees at the left all but obscure the east end. The process was already sufficiently advanced as he made the sketch, however, for him to have been unable to see the wall at the bottom of the east window, which as a consequence he omitted in all his finished compositions.

In 1801 Girtin exhibited at the Royal Academy an oil painting of Bolton Bridge. Apart from contemporary reviews which describe its 'solemn twilight', 'stern simplicity' and 'impressive grandeur' there is no record of this composition. Girtin and Loshak speculate that it perished in a fire which destroyed John Girtin's premises in 1817.[17]

Girtin 1800

18. An exceptionally close replica of this composition was with Leger Galleries 1990 no. 11.

17. Stepping Stones on the Wharfe at Bolton Abbey, c.1800

The British Museum

Fig. VI
Above Bolton Abbey, looking north
(Photograph: David Hill)

18. Stepping Stones on the Wharfe at Bolton Abbey, c.1800

National Gallery of Scotland, Edinburgh

A sketch, coloured on the spot and the finished watercolour derived from it.[18] The sketch is closely related to the sketch of Gordale Scar waterfall, also exhibited, no. 37 and both probably related to the Shepherd sketchbook in the Whitworth Art Gallery, Manchester. Records the view from the cliff opposite Bolton Priory, looking north over the river Wharfe towards Simon's Seat (fig. VI). The stepping stones still present, but obscured from this viewpoint by a footbridge. The ruins of the priory immediately beyond the left-hand edge of the composition.

The cropping of the composition to exclude Bolton priory seems extraordinarily audacious. It is as if Girtin was deliberately excluding the usual, and normally attention-grabbing, feature of the site to draw attention to the stuff of which it is ordinarily composed. Raising the literally non-descript of the world to our consciousness, as if scanning headlines was preventing our hearing the story, or finding true intimations of the profound in the text.

Fig. VII
On the Wharfe opposite Bolton Abbey
(Photograph: David Hill)

19. On the Wharfe by Bolton Priory, c.1798

The Victoria and Albert Museum, London

A view of the bluff opposite Bolton Abbey. Girtin's viewpoint in *Stepping Stones on the Whar*fe (exh. no.18) is the top of the cliffs to the right. The extensive pencil work suggests that this might be a large drawing made, and perhaps even coloured, on the spot. Given a degree of fading, it is hard to determine how bright in colour the composition might originally have been.

The watercolour represents the apotheosis of Girtin's ability to monumentalise the otherwise nondescript and unnoticeable. Here he takes no more than a steep bank by a river, which could in fact be almost anywhere except for the original title locating it on the Wharfe, and the distinctive stepped buttress which can easily be recognised at Bolton Abbey today (fig. VII). Girtin seems to have been one of the first to see any potential in such subjects, or to think that something so mundane might be worthy of attention. Its simple nature is perhaps personified in the figure of the shepherd, and the idea to represent the natural sensibility of the simply-bred such as the shepherd or, indeed, the artist. The watercolour was bought from Girtin by Edward Lascelles, possibly in 1798.[19] Girtin's achievement in this department seems to have been quickly recognised by his fellow artists. John Sell Cotman's most famous watercolours of the Greta in 1805 seem to have been inspired by his example, and Turner was probably mindful of Girtin's identification with this kind of subject when he revisited Harewood in 1808.[20] Turner adopted a similar ploy in his treatment of the same site in his famous 'England and Wales' watercolour of about 1825.[21] Although he stopped short of altogether eliminating the abbey as had Girtin, this too might have been a memory of Girtin's groundbreaking work at this site.

19. Cf p. xx.
20. Cf. Tate Gallery, London, Turner Bequest, Derbyshire sketchbook, 1808 TB CVI 88a.
21. Bolton Abbey, Yorkshire, now at the Lady Lever Art Gallery, Port Sunlight, Cheshire (National Museums and Galleries on Merseyside). Cf F Milner, Turner Paintings in Merseyside Collections, 1990, no.11.

20. Ilkley Yorkshire, c.1800

Leeds Museums and Galleries (City Art Gallery)

A view of the church with Ilkley Moor beyond, from by the river, to the south west of the church. The viewpoint today obscured by trees. Girtin probably sketched this view on his excursion to Bolton Abbey from Harewood, and Edward Lascelles was pleased enough with the subject to purchase the finished watercolour. Once again the subject is an unusual one. Girtin is certainly the first major artist and possibly one of the first artists of any kind to have thought Ilkley worthy of their attention, or capable of yielding to meaning, as here in this browned, but nevertheless powerfully austere image.

21. On the Wharfe, c.1800

Sir Nicholas Bacon

Girtin's interest in the undemonstrative in landscape has resulted in this composition remaining unidentified today. Rather than accept its traditional title of On the Wharfe near Farnley, it seems more likely that it represents a scene on the Wharfe between Ilkley and Bolton Abbey, looking towards Bolton Bridge and that the hill in the left distance is Simon's Seat. Fading has probably made the composition more severe than it might originally have been, but the material of which it is composed was always pared down to the absolutely essential even for him. No detail, flourish or convention is allowed to complicate the plain grasp of the fundamental.

Fig. VIII
Harewood Bridge and Weir
(Photograph: David Hill)

*22. **Harewood Bridge,** c.1799-1800*

Harewood House Trust

The view from the south bank of the river Wharfe, looking across the weir where a group of men is engaged in repair work. Faded almost to monochrome, but some bright colour is preserved in the detail of the figures.

Girtin was once again on his own here in his choice of subject. Few artists, if any, had made it their subject before him. Few enough, indeed, afterwards. Once again he revealed in hitherto nondescript material, significance of dramatic weight. It is a simple enough scene, of a medieval bridge and workers mending a weir. A platform and hoist has been erected to drive the piling into the river-bed. Foremen direct operations from the bank and from midstream, and a gang of men haul on the lifting rope. This activity takes place, however, against such a relentless tide of elements – the sweep of the sky reflected by the river – as to suggest the inevitability of even the doughty bridge being swept away. It is possible that the repair work was the result of flood damage (see nos. 23 and 36). The subdued colour now adds powerfully to an effect which is almost primordial, but given the brightness in the detail of the figures it seems unlikely that the effect was ever very much more colourful, merely more silvery and cool. Primordiality was Girtin's intention.

*23. **Wetherby Bridge and Mills looking across the weir,*** *c.1800-01*
Private Collection

Looking from the south bank of the river Wharfe across the weir to Wetherby mills and bridge. In Girtin's day the bridge carried the great north road across the river, and the town was an important market and posting centre. Some of the inn buildings can be made out beyond the mills. The mills ground corn and rape in the early years of the 19th century, but virtually everything in the scene has been redeveloped, except for the bridge on this downstream side.[23] Once again Girtin was working in little-frequented territory, and these two watercolours are rare records of the town from this period.[24] It is interesting that here as at Harewood Bridge (no. 22) only a few miles upstream, there is work being carried out on the weir. There are records of major floods in Yorkshire, particularly in the river Aire in 1799.[25] It seems possible that during the following summer, with the water low, Girtin recorded the damage being repaired. There is a study for this watercolour in a private collection.[26]

Fig. IX
Wetherby Bridge and Weir
(Photograph: David Hill)

*24. **Wetherby Bridge, looking through the bridge to the mills,*** *c.1800-01*

Private Collection

The view upstream through the northern arches of the bridge to the Wetherby mills. Based on a pencil sketch formerly in the collection of Lord Harewood, this watercolour seems never before to have been publicly exhibited. A better-known version is in the British Museum.[27] Close comparison of the pencil sketch and the two finished versions suggests that the present watercolour was probably the first. The relationship to the sketch and understanding of the details recorded in the sketch, e.g. the thatched roof of the building through the right arch, and the smaller arches of the old bridge both left and right,[28] is closer throughout. The composition has been refined slightly in the British Museum version. Although the bridge has been altered on this side since Girtin recorded it, and the mills have long since disappeared, the general character captured by Girtin is recognisable today, although the interesting details of women doing the laundry in the river which Girtin observed on site in his sketch, will be less frequently encountered.

22. Hitherto known as Wetherby Chapel and bridge, by mistaking the mill building beyond the weir for a chapel.
23. Interesting early photographs of the mills are included in *Wetherby: The Archives Photographs* series, compiled by Wetherby Historical Society, 1995, p.17, and an 1857 engraving from the same viewpoint as the present watercolour is reproduced in R Unwin, *Wetherby: The History of a Yorkshire Market Town,* Wetherby Historical Trust, 1986, p. 103. Both contain early 19th.C. maps of Wetherby which identify the corn and rape mills.
24. Turner sketched there in 1816 cf. Turner Bequest, Tate Gallery, TB CXLIV 8a-9.
25. Cf Radley & Simms, *Yorkshire Flooding,* 1971 p. 8.
26. G&L 348 as *Hexham Bridge.*
27. 1855-2-14-7, G&L 391i, exh V&A 1975 no. 75.
28. The medieval bridge was widened on its upstream side in 1773, and then again on the downstream side in 1826. Girtin's watercolour does, however, suggest that some widening had already taken place on the downstream side before 1826, for here we can see (as today) the smaller medieval bridge through the wider arches of a later remodelling. This is less clear in the British Museum watercolour, where one might easily read the depiction as merely odd perspective on the underside of a single, continuous arch.

25. Grimbald Bridge, near Knaresborough, c.1800

Harewood House Trust

26. Bilton Banks, near Knaresborough, c.1800

Harewood House Trust

27. Abbey Mill, Knaresborough, c.1801

Yale Center for British Art, Paul Mellon Collection

The Abbey Mill (no. 27), or more correctly Priory Mill, stands on the left bank of the river Nidd just over a mile downstream of Knaresborough Castle.A few hundred yards further downstream stands Grimbald bridge (no. 25) which carries the old Knaresborough to Wetherby road. On the opposite bank to the mill stands the weathered yellow sandstone outcrop of Grimbald Crag. Many of these subjects are represented in the Shepherd sketchbook at the Whitworth Art Gallery, Manchester, which also includes other subjects nearby such as Plompton Hall stables. In addition, sketches of related subjects survive separately including at Harewood a pencil sketch of Bilton Banks (no. 26) on the Nidd about two miles upstream of the Knaresborough Castle. All seem likely to have originated on the same excursion probably in 1800.[29]

Priory Mill is only just recognisable today having been considerably enlarged and modernised as a private house. The subject was first identified by the sixth Earl of Harewood in the 1930's when he observed that; 'There is still a tiny island where Girtin has put in a little tuft of vegetation below the mill wheel, but it has quite a respectable tree on it now'.[30] The watercolour is in remarkably fresh condition. This does not, however, it will be noted, make it even remotely demonstrative in colour. It is no more than a plain old undershot mill with a ramp leading up to it and a clump of trees beyond, painted with the coolness and clarity of a typically reticent English summer in the north. In this case it will occasion no surprise to discover that Girtin was unique here in his choice of subject.[31]

29. Subjects in the Shepherd sketchbook are Abbey Mill (G&L 437i) , the basis of the watercolour exhibited here; Grimbald Bridge (G&L 371) a thought-provokingly exact version of that exhibited here from the Harewood collection; Grimbald Crag (G&L 369) more-or-less the continuation to the left of the view of the abbey mill; a crag on the Nidd (G&L 370ii) possibly St Robert's Cave between the Abbey Mill and Grimbald Bridge – a composition which also has a remarkably close variant (G&L 370i) in the British Museum (1855-2-14-33); Plompton Hall stables (G&L 374); Village at the bend of a river (G&L 450, but cf under no. 38 below). In addition there are pencil drawings of Spofforth Castle (between Knaresborough and Wetherby) and Knaresborough Castle from the High bridge (neither in G&L) both sold from the Harewood collection at Christie's 13.7.1965 lots 165 as 'Spofforth Abbey' (sic) and 164 as 'Bilton Banks' (sic).
30. Hardie 1939 p. 93.
31. There is an amateur copy in watercolour at the Victoria and Albert Museum, London, Dyce 725, DG.8a

*28. **York Minster from the south east, Layerthorpe bridge and postern to the right,** c.1795*
The British Museum

*29. **York, Pavement,** c.1796-7, possibly exhibited RA 1797*
Private Collection, courtesy of Spink-Leger Pictures

During the 18th century York was the hub of northern society life and artists naturally gravitated there in numbers. The first York subject exhibited here appears to originate from the time of Girtin's association with Edward Dayes. It does not have the firmness of knowledge of the subject that one might expect if Girtin has studied it at first hand. The chapter house is normally firmly attached to the north side of the Minster but here floats uncertainly between its wonted place and the little church of St Cuthbert. It seems likely therefore that his information was derived from the work of another artist. However infirm the knowledge of York might be, however, Girtin was confident enough already in his knowledge of effects to set the Minster alight with morning sunlight shafting against a steely sky. Already he is laying down the foundations of his maturity.[32]

York was a major subject for Girtin on his first tour of the north in 1796 and five of his ten exhibits at the Royal Academy in 1797 were views in the city. One likely member of this group is this sparkling view of the well-known York street of Pavement. The view is quite recognisable today from near the bottom of the Shambles looking to All Saints church, although the church of St Croix to the right has long disappeared together with the market cross before All Saints. The busy scene with its picturesque and attentively observed figures is freshly preserved and we might imagine that it and its companions in the exhibition of 1797 gave Turner much-more-than-usual pause as he prepared for his own northern tour that summer. He would certainly have consulted with his friend for advice, and it can be no coincidence that Turner sketched exactly the same view of Pavement himself in 1797.[33] The subject might have been particularly significant for in both this and Turner's sketch each artist takes the trouble to notice at the left the sign of the Black Horse Inn. This is now long disappeared but was a rambling and bustling inn at the time and by no means the most expensive. It might well be that it served as a base for the two young men as they made their explorations of the city.

32. This composition was engraved as a coloured aquatint by J Hill and published by Rudolf Ackerman on 1 May 1800. York City Art Gallery has a print (R. 3770). In 1800 he repeated the composition on a larger scale and with the sun now set dramatically to the left (G&L 154ii) and this in its turn was engraved in mezzotint by S W Reynolds Ic.1823 and by T Lupton for his *Rivers of England* published on 1 August 1824. York has copies of both prints R. 3781/2, and R 2895. A c.1802 composition in the Whitworth, Manchester (G&L 486) records the view across Layerthorpe Bridge and Postern.
33. Tate Gallery, Turner Bequest, TB XXXV 66, cf. Hill 1996 p. 143.

34. Turner Bequest, Tate Gallery, TB XXXV 86, cf. Hill 1996 p. 148-9.
35. The supply and distribution of coal is one of Girtin's main themes at York (see nos. 31 & 32 below).

*30. **York Minster, south side,** 1796-7. possibly exhibited RA 1797*

Private collection

This impressive and well-preserved watercolour is likely to have been another of Girtin's 1797 Royal Academy exhibits. Once again it seems to have inspired Turner to sketch the subject himself.[34] Its impact on Turner might have been considerable for it is without doubt one of Girtin's finest architectural compositions. This is a genre for which Turner was renowned, but here Girtin's handling of detail is extraordinary throughout, with perhaps some allowance being needed for the rose window in the upper storey of the transept. But most impressive is the way in which he throws light and shade over the building to give the impression of cloud scudding across the sky. The complexity of light over the structure is as varied as one might normally expect to find over a city, and gives a sense of scale to the building and also of the forces that play over and around it. As with *York: Pavement,* one feels also that Girtin has taken real interest in his figures. The group enjoying the sun by the Minster door is particularly attractive, as is the sharply observed detail of the coalman back-hauling his load along the street.[35] Given its possible influence on Turner it is doubly interesting that this watercolour originated from Farnley Hall, the Yorkshire seat of Turner's famous patron Walter Fawkes, whose even more famous ancestor, Guy Fawkes, was born in a house not far from the viewpoint of this watercolour and was baptised in the church of St Martin le Belfry, part of which can be seen here to the left. Apart from its surmised appearance at the Royal Academy this seems to be the first occasion on which it has ever been shown publicly. Although we do not know when it came into the Farnley collection, it seems possible that Girtin might have been noticed by Fawkes before Turner.

Fig. X
York Minster: South Side
(Photograph: David Hill)

36. Although this watercolour is now at Harewood, it is a relatively late acquisition, having been bought by the Sixth Earl, probably in the 1930s.

37. Turner Bequest, Tate Gallery, TB XXXV 70, cf. Hill 1996 p. 146

***31. York Minster from the Ouse, near St Mary's Abbey,* c.*1797*[36]**

Harewood House Trust

***32. York, Ouse Bridge from downstream,* 1800**

Yale Center for British Art, Paul Mellon Collection

York Minster from the Ouse is another watercolour probably derived from Girtin's tour of 1796 that was also sketched by Turner from exactly the same spot in 1797.[37] The barge moored at the end of Marygate in the foreground is evidence of the busy river traffic of the time that brought coal up from the Humber seaports and returned laden with grain.

Coal barge traffic might not seem obvious material with which to stir the aesthetic emotions, but in 1800 he returned to the same theme, and made of it another of his masterpieces. *The Ouse Bridge, York* records the view from the King's Staith on the north bank looking upstream to the bridge and St William's chapel. All this was demolished within a few years, but for a time at the end of the eighteenth century it enjoyed a pictorial celebrity almost unsurpassed in Britain. Some commentators even compared the waterfront of York to the Grand Canal, and the Ouse Bridge to the Rialto. But while the York riverside might indeed justify comparison with Venice, at least on a good day, here Girtin is deliberately deflating its pretensions. To the right we are confronted with the muddy bank, and beyond it the detail of scuttles and quayside paraphernalia painted in lamp black as if Girtin was painting with coal, as well as making it his subject. The colour seems everywhere muted, and perhaps this was quite deliberate for the figures on the bridge present tiny dabs of the primaries of red, yellow and blue as if to assure us that the colour is as the artist intended. Nevertheless out of such material he has carved and balanced a structure of noble poise and monumentality. The details particularly reward close scrutiny. The dappled shadow on the left side of the bridge is especially noteworthy, cast by a plume of smoke rising against the low sun to the left. And at the extreme right is the detail of a small girl being frightened by a beggar. This might be easily overlooked, but one is forced to wonder what Girtin might have meant by this. The cosseted classes encountering the real world, perhaps?

33. Ripon Cathedral from Skellgate Bridge, c.1800

Blackburn Museum and Art Galleries

The view over Skellgate bridge on the Ripon to Harrogate road, looking down the river Skell to the west front of the cathedral. The view has hitherto been thought to be a *capriccio,*[38] but although new buildings and trees obscure details and prevent access to the exact viewpoint, the bridge still stands[39] and enough is visible at the site to confirm the identification.

The excursion to Ripon and nearby Fountains Abbey would be a highlight of any visit to Yorkshire, and was popular with tourists well before the end of the eighteenth century.[40] Girtin made early drawings from other artists of both Ripon and Fountains whilst still working for Dayes,[41] and visited Ripon on his first visit to the north in 1796,[42] and although nothing of Fountains of this date is known today, it is inconceivable that he would have missed it when so close.

The watercolour of Ripon exhibited here is one of several known versions of the composition. The prime version is at the Yale Center for British Art,[43] the first owner of which appears to have been none other than John Constable. The other versions are all more-or-less-weak direct copies, whose authorship ought to be reviewed critically.[44] The present example is weaker than the Yale version but varies the detail sufficiently to constitute a reworking of the composition rather than a slavish copy.

38. G&L 386, V&A 1975 no. 72 et al.
39. Although widened on its upstream side.
40. Especially after John Aislaby incorporated Fountains into the gardens of his house at Studley Royal in the early years of the century. Edward Lascelles made a tour to Ripon, Studley and Hackfall (another Aislaby garden, near Masham) in September/October 1795, cf. Account-book 189 13 September and 12 October.
41. A watercolour of Ripon based on a composition by Thomas Hearne is in the British Museum, 1878-12-28-21 (G&L 15) and another of Fountains (G&L p.208 as untr), made for James Moore was sold at Christie's 14.2.78 (52 repr) to Spink 1978 (10 not r.)
42. I would date the faded but still impressive watercolour in the National Gallery of Scotland (1012) to this tour. G&L 156 accept it only with some reserve, but it seems to me to be a fine piece, possibly sketched on the spot in pencil, and perhaps even coloured on the spot to some extent. I would compare it very closely with the large sketch of Durham, no. 4 in the present exhibition.
43. Yale Center for British Art, New Haven, USA, B1977.14.364 (G&L 386i, V&A 1975 no. 72). This is inscr: 'Girtin 1800'.
44. Leeds City Art Gallery (G&L 386ii), National Gallery of Ireland (G&L 386iii) repr., and others not catalogued by G&L, but known through photographs in the Witt library, in the collections of Sir John and Lady Witt inv. no. 1386 and Mrs I R Boda (in 1975). Perhaps we should wonder if one of the copies might even be by Constable!

*34. **Fountains Abbey, the great east window from the presbytery,** c.1799*

Sheffield Galleries and Museums Trust

The view from the floor of the presbytery across the high altar to the south transept of the chapel of nine altars. A rainbow through the great east window. Visitors to the site today will be entertained to locate Girtin's viewpoint. He was perched on the lip of a stone coffin set into the floor of the presbytery. This is the only point from which the rearing perspective of the masonry can be obtained. Given that his failing health hangs like a cloud over the short story of his life it is thought-provoking to find him sketching with not one but both feet in the grave. One might feel at least a little self-conscious in emulating him today, and there seems no doubt that he meant us to discover this, for he hints strongly at the particularity of his viewpoint by situating the blue and red floor tiles of the high altar podium right before our eyes along the bottom edge of the composition.

Fig. XI
East End of Fountains Abbey
(Photograph: David Hill)

Fig. XII
Richmond from Station Bridge: Autumn
(Photograph: David Hill)

35. Richmond Castle and town from the south east, 1796-7

Private Collection, courtesy of Agnew's, London

The view is perfectly recognisable today and is perhaps best viewed from the Station bridge. This was not built, however, until 1848 to link the new-built railway station with the town, and Girtin's vantage-point must have been the high right bank of the river at this point. In 1796 Girtin must have had to work quite hard to obtain this view by walking round from the high bridge upstream.

In the 18th century the market town of Richmond with its spectacular cluster of castle and houses hanging over the river was outrivalled in the north only by Durham for its picturesque celebrity. It was naturally a major subject for Girtin on his tour of 1796,[45] and warranted a return *c.*1800.[46] In this case, however, it will be observed that Girtin's pictorial imagination ran away with him a little. From this height above the river it would be impossible to see a reflection of the castle keep. By the time that the composition was engraved for publication in 1798[47] the potential embarrassment was recognised and the errant reflection removed.

45. A sketch and a finished watercolour survive recording the view from upstream. Girtin & Loshak (252i & ii) date these to 1798, but there seems no reason to doubt that the sketch was made in 1796 and that the watercolour followed soon after.
46. Watercolour at Leeds City Art Gallery, G&L 390 inscr 'Girtin 1800'.
47. John Walker, *Copper-Plate Magazine,* 1 November 1798. Walker seems to have felt free to reinvent many other details of the watercolour, besides.

Fig. XIII
Packhorse Bridge, Hawes
(Photograph: David Hill)

*36. **Hawes, Yorkshire,** 1800*

Birmingham Museums and Art Gallery

Showing the view looking upstream from near Holm Bridge to the old packhorse bridge and waterfall beyond. The bridge and cottage beyond are still recognisable, despite alterations. together with the lean-to shed at the right. All else at the right has been rebuilt but the watercourse feeding the mills through the right-hand side of the bridge and running along the top of the wall at the right is still traceable. It is shown here broken and spilling water back into the river. The details are clear in the pencil sketch on which this is based, also at Birmingham.[48] One is forced to wonder what can have happened to cause the mill's life-blood to be thus draining away. Perhaps there had been a flood such as that suggested by the watercolours of Wetherby and Harewood bridge. The present exhibit is the prime version of a number of versions.[49] As in other cases with Girtin, the relationship of the versions would benefit from critical comparative review.

In 1800 Edward Lascelles' personal account books record that he made two tours both of which might be relevant to Girtin. On 16 July he recorded his 'Expenses to the Lakes, post Horses &c £5.10.0' and on 7 August 'Expenses into Craven, Post Horses &c £5.5.0'.[50] It is possible that these entries record the same journey from Harewood, since the Craven Dales area of Yorkshire lies *en route* from Harewood to the Lake District. It seems more than a little coincidental that Girtin made numerous sketches of subjects in this area at this time, and it seems tempting to wonder whether he might not have accompanied his patron on this tour. We have no idea what route was taken but it is inevitable that such a journey would include some of the Yorkshire Dales, and could easily have included all the Dales and Lakes sites that we know Girtin to have visited around 1800: Ripon, Richmond, Middleham, Hawes, Lodore Falls, the Malham area, Gordale and finally perhaps Bolton Abbey and Ilkley.[51]

However this may be, the present watercolour places him in Wensleydale in 1800 or thereabouts. It is, however, more than a little puzzling that there are no other known Wensleydale subjects from his hand at this time apart from the pencil drawings of Middleham in the Shepherd sketchbook. He was familiar at least with one of the dale's principal landmarks for he had painted Bolton Castle during his time with Edward Dayes.[52] We have already noted cases of Girtin's original approach to subject-matter, and here, as with other subjects, one will be hard pressed to find many, if any, earlier representations. But to represent a tour to Wensleydale with a couple of sketches of Middleham and another, however interesting, of Hawes, and to ignore Aysgarth Falls, Bolton Castle, and Hardraw Force seems original to the point of being obtuse. Perhaps there is material yet to come to light.

48. G&L 392i, Birmingham City Art Gallery 39/29.
49. G&L 392iii (Private collection ex Sotheby's 19.3.1981 lot 127), G&L 392iv (Bacon collection); G&L 392v (Ashmolean Museum, Oxford).
50. Account book 191. It is perhaps worth giving a resume of Edward Lascelles' recorded tours, as others might be relevant to his association with Girtin, or even with other artists: 1795 to Sussex cf. 189 2 May and 30 June; to the Lakes cf. 189 6 Sept; to Ripon, Welbeck, Studley and Hackfall, cf 189 13 Sept, 4 and 12 Oct; 1796 to Brighton cf. 189, 9 and 28 Oct; 1798 to Liverpool &c cf. 191 22 Sept; 1799 to Hampton Court Herefordshire and a tour of the river Wye , cf. 191 20, 24 Aug. and to Scarborough cf. 191 6 September; 1800 and 1801 to the Lakes and Craven as detailed above. I cannot resist mentioning that the 1799 account also records the generous (and suspiciously unexplained) payment of one guinea to the 'Maid at H[ampton] Court' (191 26 August).
51. Lascelles went to Craven again in 1801 cf. account book 189 21 Sept 1801 'To Expenses to Craven post Horses &c £6.6.0', but by this time Girtin was preparing to go to Paris.
52. G&L 24, Oxford, Ashmolean Museum (DBB 699).

53. See Edward J Nygren: *James Ward's Gordale Scar: An Essay in the Sublime,* catalogue of the exhibition at the Tate Gallery, 1982.
54. One pencil sketch of Kirkby Malham, not in G&L, approx. 6 x 8 ins and inscr: 'Kirkby near Malham' was with Leger Galleries (attrib. Henry Edridge) in 1984. Susan Morris reidentified the finished watercolour G&L 447, private collection ex Sotheby's 10.10.1974 lot 39, from 'Horton' as it was then known, to Kirkby Malham. The view is perfectly recognisable today, entering the village from the south. It is also worth recording here that a well-preserved copy of this, most certainly not by Girtin, survives at Blackburn Art Gallery (534). In addition, the Shepherd sketchbook contains a sketch (G&L 433i) of some village houses and barns inscr: 'near Malham, Kirkby', but I cannot identify anything at Kirkby Malham today with those here. This sketch formed the basis of the finished watercolour (G&L 433ii) at the British Museum 1855-2-14-5, known as 'Kirkby Priory, Yorkshire'. Interestingly the verso of the Shepherd sketchbook page is inscr 'Kirkby Church' which indicates that the private collection drawing was removed from there.

37. Gordale Scar waterfall, c.1800

The British Museum,

A small sketch coloured on the spot, recording the view of the lower falls. So close in size and colouring to the sketch of *Stepping Stones on the Wharfe* (no. 17) as certainly to have been made on the same tour. It seems further likely to be related to drawings made in the same area in the Shepherd sketchbook at the Whitworth Art Gallery Manchester (see below). It is probable that most of these subjects were made in 1800 given their relationship to dated finished works, and possible that these were made in the company of Edward Lascelles who made a tour to Craven and the Lakes in that year (see under no.36).

Allowing for rock falls over the years Girtin's sketch seems sensitively as well as delicately observed. It compares well with James Ward's rigorous studies made in 1811,[53] and yet constructs a sparkle of tonal droplets that comes close to taking on the actual form of its subject as well as its appearance. That said, Gordale Scar is one of the most extraordinary phenomena in Britain. It is a limestone gorge with overhanging walls over three hundred feet high. Above this fall is another, considerably higher, that bursts through a natural rock arch, and from a viewpoint slightly further to the right both falls can be seen at the same time. This small sketch seems in this light to be a rather strangely oblique record of the experience. In fact, as with Wensleydale, his surviving record of the area would seem absurdly obtuse if it were all that he originally made. All that survives besides this is two sketches of Kirkby Malham, a relatively obscure village in the dale when compared to Malham itself and its world-famous three hundred foot high Malham Cove. The effect of wilful obscurity is only compounded by the fact that amongst the finished work, even if other sketches were made, Girtin seems to have selected only Kirkby Malham.[54]

Fig. XIV
Gordale Scar Waterfall
(Photograph: David Hill)

55. G&L 426i.
56. Farington Diary 24 March 1807.
57. G&L p.42.
58. Morris 1986 p.21.
59. Shepherd sketchbook, G&L 425. A sketch at the British Museum (G&L 431) is also probably from the Shepherd sketchbook and has hitherto been known as Brough. This is impossible since the sea is visible in the right distance. The mistake is based on a misreading of the inscription which, so far as I can make it our, reads: 'The House and castle very/ Bright The ..[?] lighter'. The view shows Mulgrave Park and Castle from near Epsyke farm. The church visible to the left is Lythe church. Another sketch in the Shepherd sketchbook G&L 450 shows a village on a bend of a river and seems to me more likely to be a subject in the Whitby/Sandsend area, or perhaps even Devon, than near Knaresborough as is usually thought. It is, however, such an unprepossessing subject that we ought best to consider why Girtin sketched it at all.
60. A page removed from the Shepherd sketchbook and now untraced but recorded in an inscription.
61. G&L 346, exh V&A 1975 no. 62, as Tynemouth, private collection ex Sotheby's 13 November 1997 lot 44.

*38. **Sandsend, Yorkshire,** 1802*

Yale Center for British Art, Paul Mellon Collection

Sandsend is a tiny village at the end of the beach about three miles north of Whitby on the north east coast of Yorkshire. The watercolour is based on a pencil sketch in the Shepherd sketchbook at the Whitworth Art Gallery in Manchester.[55] Girtin went to Sandsend as a result of visiting Lord Mulgrave at nearby Mulgrave Park. Some years after Girtin's death Lord Mulgrave 'spoke with much regard of the memory of Girtin, the Artist, who was with him a little time at Mulgrave castle – he thought him a good natured, open-dispositioned man'.[56] He also mentioned that Girtin clearly 'laboured under the Symptoms of an Asthma which not long afterwards killed him.' We do not know exactly when this tour took place, but Girtin and Loshak suggest the spring of 1801,[57] and Susan Morris suggests that he extended this visit to take in Northumberland besides.[58]

Fig. XV
Sandsend
(Photograph: David Hill)

The view of Sandsend is perfectly recognisable today. Most of the cottages are still present, and many little altered. The bridge carrying the coast road to Staithes and Redcar has disappeared to be replaced by a modern bridge more or less at Girtin's viewpoint. Nevertheless is seems once again that Girtin has made a less-than-obvious selection out of the options available to him in the neighbourhood. He sketched Mulgrave Castle in the woods,[59] a view from the Gravel caves,[60] and the view down the beach to Whitby,[61] but there is no record of Whitby itself with its harbour and ancient abbey, nor of the spectacular cliff scenery to the north of Sandsend. The fact that the roaring waves of the North Sea were only yards from his back as he sketched this suggests that he was deliberately selecting out the modest and the obscure. Again it is a subject so modest that Girtin seems to have been the first to think of it.

39. Guisborough Priory, 1801

National Gallery of Scotland, Edinburgh

Guisborough[62] is less than twenty miles north of Whitby and Girtin must have visited the priory whilst staying with Lord Mulgrave at Mulgrave castle (see exh. no. 38). He sketched the ruins in the Shepherd sketchbook at the Whitworth Art Gallery[63] and the drawing provided the basis of two finished watercolours, the present example which was bought by Edward Lascelles, and another recorded as being in the possession of one S Ribault in 1823[64] and now in the Tate Gallery in London.[65]

62. English Heritage perpetuate a distinction between the spelling of Gisborough (Priory) and Guisborough (town).
63. G&L 430i.
64. A fragment of an 1823 exhibition list for Cooke's Gallery at 9 Soho Square, London, collected for some drawings of ships on it by Turner, survives in the Yale Center for British Art, New Haven USA (B1975.4.1761). One of the items included in the list, however, is '12 Gisborough Abbey, Yorkshire. In the possession of S Ribault Esq. T Girtin Died 1802'. This would at least suggest the authenticity of both versions, since the present version was at that time still in the Lascelles family collection.
65. G&L 430ii. The two versions are not quite identical. The present version is slightly more highly finished, the Tate version has some relatively unfinished parts, especially e.g. the spire at the left, but has also sought to develop greater drama in the sky, although the original effect is now somewhat faded. Girtin's visit to Guisborough also gave rise to another composition of the east end from the north east with Roseberry Topping in the distance. No sketch is recorded but there is a finished watercolour in the Bacon collection (G&L 452), a copy in the Yale Center (B1975. 3.1208) and an oil version (the only oil attributed to Girtin with any confidence) also at the Yale Center (B1978.20).
66. The curious might care to consider the figures lower right. A man in a blue coat seems to be shooting with a pistol at a pear balanced on the girl's head. Some explanation seems required.

The great east end of Guisborough Priory is the only substantial part now standing, and Girtin's watercolour records the inner face as seen from the graveyard of the parish church. Edward Lascelles might have had a special interest in the subject for his family were long associated with north Yorkshire and his 13th century ancestors were early benefactors of the priory. The relatively conventional sublimity of the composition constitutes something of an exception for Girtin at this time. A visit to the site however provides food for thought. The graves in the foreground represent the rather eccentric piles of old memorial stones that are strewn around the graveyard. The parish church of St Nicholas still stands, but must have been dwarfed by its neighbour during the hey-day of the priory. On site one realises that Girtin is gazing at the priory from common territory, looking over the boundary wall of the graveyard into the priory grounds. In selecting to sketch from this viewpoint he might well have intended us to consider ruined ambitions in the form of the priory, contrasted with still-sustained modesty in the form of the parish church.[66]

Fig. XVI
East end of Guisborough Priory from St Nicholas' church yard.
(Photograph: David Hill)

THOMAS GIRTIN: Genius in the North

Exhibition at Harewood House, Yorkshire, 12 March - 13 June 1999

LIST OF EXHIBITS

1. ***Harewood House from the South East,*** *1801*
Watercolour, $24^{3/4}$ x $38^{1/2}$ ins, 627 x 978 mm
Harewood House Trust
G&L 434, V&A 1975 no. 83

2. John Opie
Portrait of Thomas Girtin, *c.1800*
Oil on canvas, $29^{3/4}$ x $24^{3/4}$ ins, 755 x 630 mm
National Portrait Gallery, London (882)

3. ***Dunstanburgh Castle, Northumberland, in a thunderstorm*** *c.1795*
Watercolour, $6^{1/2}$ x $8^{7/8}$ ins, 166 x 225 mm
The Visitors of the Ashmolean Museum, Oxford (717)
G&L 72, V&A 1975 no. 6

4. ***Durham Cathedral and Castle from above Framwellgate Bridge,*** *1796*
Watercolour, $10^{1/8}$ x $15^{5/8}$ ins 258 x 366 mm
Birmingham Museums and Art Gallery (220'53)
G&L 237

5. ***Durham Cathedral and Castle from above Framwellgate Bridge,*** *1799*
Watercolour, $16^{3/8}$ x $21^{1/8}$ ins, 416 x 537 mm
Inscr: (on weir) 'T Girtin 1799'
The Whitworth Art Gallery, University of Manchester
G&L 158iii, V&A 1975 no. 16

6. ***An Estuary Scene, probably in Devon,*** *c.1801*
Watercolour, $8^{7/8}$ x $16^{3/4}$ ins, 225 x 425 mm
Inscr: (l.l.) 'Girtin'
Harewood House Trust
Borenius no.309, G&L 256

7. John Hoppner
Portrait of Edward Lascelles, *1797*
Oil on canvas, $35^{3/8}$ x $27^{3/8}$ ins, 899 x 695 mm
Harewood House Trust

8. ***Temple in Harewood Park,*** *c.1798*
Watercolour, $11^{7/8}$ x 11 ins, 302 x 279 mm
Yale Center for British Art, Paul Mellon Collection
B1975.3.1193
G&L 269

9. ***Ships in a Harbour,*** *c.1798*
Watercolour, $11^{1/4}$ x $10^{1/4}$ ins, 286 x 260 mm
Inscr: (ll.) 'Girtin'
Harewood House Trust
G&L where d. 1800

10. ***Ships in a Harbour,*** *c.1798*
Pencil, 7 x $7^{1/2}$ ins, 180 x 190 mm
Inscr: (on old mount) 'Shipping at Dover'
Harewood House Trust
Not in G&L

11. ***Harewood House from the South West,*** *1801*
Watercolour, $24^{3/4}$ x $37^{3/4}$ ins, 629 x 959 mm
Harewood House Trust
G&L 435, V&A 1975 no. 84

12. ***Harewood House from the South East,*** *c.1797*
Pencil, $7^{5/8}$ x $14^{1/4}$ ins, 194 x 362 mm
Inscr: (lc) 'Harewood'
Yale Center for British Art, Paul Mellon Collection, B1975.3.1192
G&L 268

13. ***Lodore Falls, Derwentwater,*** *c.1800*
Watercolour, $21^{1/8}$ x $17^{1/2}$ ins, 535 x 446 mm
Inscr: (l.c.) 'Girtin'
The Visitors of the Ashmolean Museum, Oxford (745)
G&L 432ii, V&A 1975 no. 82

14. ***Kirkstall Abbey with a canal barge, evening,*** *1802*
Watercolour, $12^{1/2}$ x $20^{1/2}$ ins, 315 x 520 mm
Inscr: (ll.) 'T Girtin 1802'
Private Collection, courtesy of Agnew's, London
G&L 448ii; Agnew's 1982 no. 29

15. ***Kirkstall Abbey from the bridge, morning,*** *c.1802*
Watercolour, $12^{1/2}$ x $20^{1/2}$ ins, 317 x 520 mm
The Victoria and Albert Museum, London (405-1885)
G&L 414, V&A 1975 no. 79.

16. ***Bolton Abbey, the east end from across the river Wharfe,*** *1800*
Watercolour, $12^{3/4}$ x $18^{3/4}$ ins, 324 x 477 mm
Inscr: (ll.) 'Girtin 1800'
Leeds Museums and Art Galleries (City Art Gallery) (16/51)
G&L 376ii, V&A 1975 no. 70

*17. **Stepping Stones on the Wharfe at Bolton Abbey,** c.1800*
Watercolour, $5\frac{5}{8}$ x 8 ins, 142 x 202 mm
Inscr: (ll.) 'above Bolton'
The British Museum, 1855-2-14-10
G&L 441i, V&A 1975 no. 86

*18. **Stepping Stones on the Wharfe at Bolton Abbey,** c.1800*
Watercolour, $12\frac{7}{8}$ x $20\frac{1}{2}$ ins, 327 x 518 mm
National Gallery of Scotland, Edinburgh
G&L 441ii, V&A 1975 no. 87

*19. **On the Wharfe by Bolton Priory,** c.1798*
Watercolour over pencil, $18\frac{1}{2}$ x $24\frac{1}{4}$ ins, 470 x 616 mm
The Victoria and Albert Museum, London (FA 380)
G&L 270, V&A 1975 no. 42

*20. **Ilkley Yorkshire,** c.1800*
Watercolour, 12 x $20\frac{3}{8}$ ins, 305 x 518 mm
Inscr: (verso) 'Mr Lascelles'
Leeds Museums and Galleries (City Art Gallery)
G&L 442; V&A 1975 no. 88

*21. **On the Wharfe,** c.1800*
Watercolour, $12\frac{1}{2}$ x $20\frac{3}{4}$ ins, 316 x 527 mm
Private Collection
G&L 443; V&A 1975 no. 89

*22. **Harewood Bridge,** c.1799-1800*
Watercolour $14\frac{3}{4}$ x 25 ins, 375 x 635 mm
Harewood House Trust
G&L 368, V&A 1975 no. 69, Hill 1995 p. 40

*23. **Wetherby Bridge and Mills looking across the weir,** c.1799-1800*
Watercolour $12\frac{1}{2}$ x $20\frac{1}{2}$ ins, 318 x 521 mm
Private Collection
Not in G&L, Christie's 20 November 1984 lot 102

*24. **Wetherby Bridge, looking through the bridge to the mills,** c.1799-1800*
Watercolour 13 x $20\frac{1}{2}$ ins, 330 x 521 mm
Private Collection
G&L 391ii

*25. **Grimbald Bridge, near Knaresborough,** c.1800*
Pencil, $4\frac{1}{2}$ x $6\frac{7}{8}$ ins, 114 x 175 mm
Harewood House Trust
G&L 372, Hill 1995 p. 34

*26. **Bilton Banks, near Knaresborough,** c.1800*
Pencil $4\frac{1}{2}$ x $6\frac{1}{2}$ ins, 114 x 165 mm
Harewood House Trust
G&L 373 as 'Bilton Bridge', Hill 1995 p. 35

*27. **Abbey Mill, Knaresborough,** c.1801*
Watercolour $12\frac{3}{4}$ x $21\frac{3}{4}$ ins, 324 x 552 mm
Inscr: (verso) 'Mr Reynolds Poland St No. 48[?]'
Yale Center for British Art, Paul Mellon Collection, B1975.4.1925
G&L 437ii, Morris 1986 no. 83

*28. **York Minster from the south east, Layerthorpe bridge and postern to the right,** c.1795*
Watercolour, $8\frac{1}{2}$ x $11\frac{7}{8}$ ins, 217 x 299 mm
The British Museum, 1855-2-14-11
G&L 154i where d.1796

*29. **York, Pavement,** c.1796-7, possibly exhibited RA 1797*
Watercolour $10\frac{3}{4}$ x $14\frac{3}{4}$ ins, 273 x 375 mm
Private Collection, courtesy of Spink-Leger Pictures
G&L 383 where d. c.1800, Leger 1987 no. 10, Hill 1996 p. 143

*30. **York Minster, south side,** 1796-7*
Possibly exhibited RA 1797
Watercolour 18 x $22\frac{1}{2}$ ins, 457 x 567 mm
Private Collection
G&L 181

*31. **York Minster from the Ouse, near St Mary's Abbey,** c.1797*
Watercolour, $13\frac{3}{8}$ x $19\frac{1}{4}$ ins, 340 x 489 mm
Harewood House Trust
G&L 190, Hill 1995 p.38

*32. **York, Ouse Bridge from downstream,** 1800*
Watercolour $12\frac{15}{16}$ x $20\frac{5}{8}$ ins, 329 x 524 mm
Inscr: (l.c.) 'Girtin 1800'
Yale Center for British Art, Paul Mellon Collection, B1977.14.363
G&L 382i, V&A 1975 no. 71, Morris 1986 no. 77

*33. **Ripon Cathedral from Skellgate Bridge,** c.1800*
Watercolour, $10\frac{1}{4}$ x $16\frac{1}{4}$ ins, 265 x 415 mm
Blackburn Museum and Art Galleries (353)
G&L 386iv

*34. **Fountains Abbey, the great east window from the presbytery,** c.1799*
Watercolour, $18\frac{1}{4}$ x $12\frac{5}{8}$ ins, 464 x 321 mm
Sheffield Galleries and Museums Trust (2283)
G&L 249, V&A 1975 no. 34

*35. **Richmond Castle and town from the south east,** 1796-7*
Watercolour $14\frac{3}{4}$ x $19\frac{1}{2}$ ins, 375 x 495 mm
Private Collection, courtesy of Agnew's, London
G&L 235; Agnew's 1993 no. 29

*36. **Hawes, Yorkshire,** 1800*
Watercolour $14\frac{3}{16}$ x $12\frac{9}{16}$ ins, 361 x 319 mm
Inscr: 'Girtin 1800'
Birmingham Museums and Art Gallery 1'10
G&L 392ii, V&A 1975 no. 76

*37. **Gordale Scar waterfall,** c.1800*
Watercolour over pencil, $5\frac{3}{8}$ x $7\frac{5}{8}$ ins, 137 x 194 mm
Inscr: (lr.) 'Gordale Scar'
The British Museum, 1855-2-14-19
G&L 445, V&A 1975 no. 91

*38. **Sandsend, Yorkshire,** 1802*
Watercolour over pencil, $12\frac{1}{2}$ x $20\frac{7}{8}$ ins, 318 x 530 mm
Inscr: (lr.) 'Girtin 1802'
Yale Center for British Art, Paul Mellon Collection, 1977.14.365
G&L 426ii, Morris 1986 no. 89

*39. **Guisborough Priory,** 1801*
Watercolour over pencil, 26 x 19 ins, 660 x 483 mm
Inscr: (ll.) 'Girtin 1801'
National Gallery of Scotland, Edinburgh (1385)
G&L 430iii